# LATINX TEENS

# LATINX TEENS

U.S. Popular Culture on the Page, Stage, and Screen

## Trevor Boffone and Cristina Herrera

THE UNIVERSITY OF
ARIZONA PRESS

TUCSON

The University of Arizona Press
www.uapress.arizona.edu

© 2022 by The Arizona Board of Regents
All rights reserved. Published 2022

ISBN-13: 978-0-8165-4275-8 (paperback)

Cover design by Leigh McDonald
Cover image © rawpixel

Library of Congress Cataloging-in-Publication Data
Names: Boffone, Trevor, author. | Herrera, Cristina, 1978– author.
Title: Latinx teens : U.S. popular culture on the page, stage, and screen / Trevor
 Boffone and Cristina Herrera.
Other titles: Latinx pop culture.
Description: Tucson : University of Arizona Press, 2022. | Series: Latinx pop culture
 | Includes bibliographical references and index.
Identifiers: LCCN 2021041163 | ISBN 9780816542758 (paperback)
Subjects: LCSH: Hispanic American teenagers. | Hispanic Americans in popular
 culture. | Arts and teenagers.
Classification: LCC E184.S75 B64 2022 | DDC 305.8680835/073—dc23
LC record available at https://lccn.loc.gov/2021041163

Printed in the United States of America
♾ This paper meets the requirements of ANSI/NISO Z39.48-1992 (Permanence of
Paper).

For all the teenage Latinx trailblazers, especially Emma González, for making our world better, kinder, and safer for all.

# CONTENTS

# ACKNOWLEDGMENTS

We began writing this book in summer 2020, a time when the world was battling the COVID-19 pandemic. Separated from our families, students, friends, and colleagues, we channeled our fears into the writing of this book, creating the type of book we wish we had when we were younger, one that provided us an outlet to channel our rage at, well, all the things. Coauthoring a book was a first for both of us, and, as always, there was a learning curve. We are grateful to a number of individuals who have energized our work through the years. As always, it takes a village. While our names might grace the cover of this book, we were not alone.

We want to extend our heartfelt thanks and appreciation to Arturo and Frederick Luis Aldama, series editors extraordinaires. From the book's inception, Arturo and Fede offered us the kindest and most encouraging words. We often remarked to each other that this book never felt like work because we were having so much fun writing it, and this energy was fueled by the Aldama brothers. Thank you.

We couldn't ask for a better editor than Kristen Buckles and the rest of the stellar editorial team at the University of Arizona Press. We thank our copy editor, Brie Aragaki, for her care in working on the manuscript. Their professionalism and enthusiasm have been unparalleled.

Thanks to the external reviewers whose thorough feedback has surely improved this book.

Cristina: This book has been a labor of love. Beginning with a phone call with Frederick Luis Aldama, who said "you should write this book," this project has easily been the smoothest, most validating experience of co-authoring. I have my brother from another mother, Trevor, to thank for this. Thank you, hermano, for your sharp eye, your energy, your amazing skills, and your cute kitty photos when I needed a break. There's nobody else I'd rather work with than you!

As always, I have a sizable army of amazing colleagues and friends who have stood the test of time. Big Califas-sized abrazos to all of you and to anyone I have missed; I owe you big time: Gabriella Gutiérrez y Muhs, Ramon Sanchez, Maria Lopes, Rosa Toro, Larissa Mercado-López, Laura Alamillo, Jennifer Randles, Andrew Jones, Patricia Pérez, Marisela Chávez, Magdalena Barrera, Lourdes Alberto, Eliza Rodríguez y Gibson, Ella Diaz, Yolanda Doub, Shane Moreman, Jenny Banh, Takkara Brunson, Davorn Sisavath, R. Joseph Rodríguez, Samina Najmi, Melanie Hernández, Kathleen Godfrey, William Arce, Jaime Rodríguez-Matos, John Beynon, Marci McMahon, Cathryn Merla-Watson, Amrita Das, Naida Saavedra, Marta López-Garza, Marion Rohrleitner, Claire Massey, Rebeca Burciaga, Sandra Ruiz, Romeo Guzmán, Carissa García, Gina Sandí-Díaz, Elvia Rodríguez, and my extended Fresno State family, particularly Drs. Xuanning Fu and Bernadette Muscat, for their support.

Last, but never, ever least, I owe so much to my family. My beloved Kris has provided the much-needed refuge and security I've needed. Gracias, mi amor. Thank you to my other half, Elena, for being my best friend ever. Gracias to my mother, Serafina, and, as always to my furry daughters, Carmelita, Cindy, and Cleo, for teaching me unconditional love. While working on this book, our beloved basset hound, Gus, crossed the rainbow bridge, joining our dearly departed fur babies who preceded him: Minnie, Lucy, Hazel, Sam, and Otto. Life isn't the same without you. Every day I miss my late abuelos, Papá Tomás and Mamá Chonita, and my late in-laws, Robin and Roland Kunkel. This book is for them. Gracias. Thank you.

Trevor: I've known for years that I wanted to co-author a book with Cristina, but I was convinced that she would think I had lost my mind if I suggested it to her. So I kept quiet. And then Frederick Luis Aldama entered the picture. He told us that we should write a book together on Latinx youth culture. Before Cristina could respond, I came clean—this was always something I wanted to do. Our phone meeting with Frederick ended, and, like the good chismosos we are, we both tried to call each other. It didn't take any convincing for us both to dive into the deep end and begin writing this book during summer 2020. The world felt like it was falling apart around us, but we had each other. As we spent long days in self-isolation at home, we relied on each other to take our minds off of the pandemic and racial injustice continuing to sweep across the nation. While we believed there was an audience for this book, we both knew that the two people who needed it most were the two of us. I say all of this because Cristina Herrera is exactly the co-conspirator I had always dreamed of when I started grad school. Co-editing *Nerds, Goths, Geeks, and Freaks: Outsiders in Chicanx and Latinx Young Adult Literature* was one of the most fulfilling scholarly experiences I've had, and the process of co-writing *Latinx Teens* was no different. I owe so much gratitude to mi hermana mayor Cristina for being the best collaborator I could ask for.

Of course, I owe thanks to a number of scholars who have supported my work throughout the years and especially during the pandemic. I give special thanks to Carla Della Gatta, Ella Diaz, Barrie Gelles, Patricia Herrera, Sarah Jerasa, Laura MacDonald, Claire M. Massey, Marci R. McMahon, Andrew Joseph Pegoda, Rachel Afi Quinn, Eliza Rodríguez y Gibson, Gina Sandí-Díaz, and Bryan M. Vandevender. Moreover, I am indebted to the support of my core creative community: Kevin Becerra, Ebony Cooksey, Freddy Davalos, Guadalís Del Carmen, Nelson Díaz-Marcano, Franky D. Gonzalez, Sarah Humphrey, Joshua Myles Inocéncio, Jasminne Mendez, Lupe Méndez, Emilio Rodriguez, Steward Savage, Mica Segal de la Garza, Abigail Vega, and Matt Wasson. I also thank my students at Bellaire High who have changed my life and kept me hip (or as hip as I can be!).

I thank my partner, Kayla, for always supporting my work and especially this project. These projects don't happen in a vacuum, and this book wouldn't be possible without her support. Thank you! Lastly, this book would not have been possible without my research assistant, Teddy HoneyBear, who kept me company during the long writing sessions (tons of cuddles and purrs). Later I received funding to hire a second research assistant, Pickles, whose presence was invaluable as we revised our manuscript and prepared it for production. Thank you, Teddy and Pickles!

# LATINX TEENS

Introduction

# LATINX TEENS

## U.S. Popular Culture from *Spider-Man* to *In the Heights*

During Super Bowl LIV on February 2, 2020, pop mega superstars Shakira and Jennifer Lopez, featuring Bad Bunny, performed a half-time show that is difficult to capture in one word, but if one such word exists, it is *mesmerizing*. From its political critique featuring children in cages to the explosive dance moves that could only be performed by Shakira and J.Lo, one thing is certain: Latinidad was fully on display, and, not surprisingly, in the days and weeks ahead, newspapers and magazines alike would print op-eds and personal essays from writers who were dazzled by one of the most electric halftime shows ever, a show in which not one, but two, Latinas took center stage. As Latinx studies scholars, we could not help but celebrate their performance for its daring, political, and electrifying qualities. For us, what was equally significant is that children were on the stage as well, most notably J.Lo's own kids, who performed some dance numbers of their own. The cages that held these children were beyond symbolic; instead, they alluded to the actual cages and detention centers that imprison migrant children on U.S. soil, a result of inhumane immigration policies intended to "protect the border."

While it may seem counterproductive to begin a book about Latinx adolescence and popular culture with a commentary on our love of all things J.Lo/Shakira/Bad Bunny, we highlight this halftime performance—already an iconic Latinx cultural moment—to state what is obvious but necessary to utter aloud: Latinx performers are always capable of drawing immense popularity, even more so when their displays convey sociocultural critiques. Merging the creative with the political, we insist, is a hallmark of Latinx performance, yet it is important to note that the halftime show's political commentary would have been missing had it not been for the presence of the young people. Despite the significance of the children's presence and their own important contributions to this charged performance, subsequent praise for J.Lo, Shakira, and Bad Bunny focalized the adults and *their* attack on Trumpian politics, suggesting the inability of young people to make astute commentary on anti-immigrant sentiment. This could not be further from the truth, as this book attests. What about Latinx youth? we ask. When can they get center stage? What can Latinx youth contribute to these critical conversations on culture, politics, identity, and representation? This book attempts to answer these questions.

Rewind to 2018, when yet another Spider-Man film swung into movie theaters. This one, much like its predecessors, had all of the features of the comic franchise. A nerdy, scrawny teenage boy gets bitten by a mutated spider, develops superpowers, struggles with his new identity, and defeats the villain. But something was different about this Spider-Man. Miles Morales, this Spider-Man for the twenty-first century, was Black and spoke Spanish. *Spider-Man: Into the Spider-Verse* quite literally rewrote the narrative of one of comic book history's most famous superheroes. Working alongside Spider-Man figures from across the franchise's history, including Peter Parker, Miles Morales defeats Doctor Octopus, all the while positioning his Afro-Latinx identity as an essential aspect of his Spidey senses. Although casual observers may dismiss the importance of an Afro-Latinx Spider-Man—a superhero for a new era—the franchise's spider-verse offering gave Spanish-speaking kids across the United States a space to see themselves represented in pop culture's most mainstream place— cinema. That this new Spider-Man was a Black Latino was even more significant, given the anti-Blackness that has historically plagued both the Latinx community and U.S. culture at large. *Spider-Man: Into the Spider-Verse* became the Latinx community's answer to *Black Panther* (2018) and demonstrated that Latinx teens can also be superheroes. Spider-Man doesn't have to be just Peter Parker. There is room for others to don the iconic spider suit. There is room for a Spider-Man of color, one who speaks Spanish and negotiates his racial identity alongside his newfound role as a superhero. There is room for Miles Morales and the millions of Afro-Latinx teens just like him who populate the United States and make significant contributions not only to Latinx popular culture but, perhaps most significantly, to mainstream U.S. popular culture as well.

While Jennifer Lopez and Shakira used the world's biggest stage to draw attention to the humanitarian crisis on the U.S.-Mexico border and Miles Morales situated the Spider-Man franchise as a space for Afro-Latinx representation, novelists, playwrights, and screenwriters alike have been inserting Latinx teenagers into the twenty-first-century narrative. Although Latinx teens have always been found in U.S. pop culture, the twenty-first century has seen a more concerted effort to center Latinidad in mainstream U.S. culture. The publishing powerhouse Knopf published Erika L. Sánchez's debut novel, *I Am Not Your Perfect Mexican Daughter* (2017), an enormously successful young adult (YA) book that has been adapted for the stage and is in the works for the screen. In television, *Party of Five* (2020) set the whiteness of the show's original 1990s family aside; the reboot instead saw five young Latinxs dealing with the immediate aftermath of their parents' unexpected deportation to Mexico. Lin-Manuel Miranda and Quiara Alegría Hudes's mega-popular, Tony-winning Broadway musical *In the Heights* (2008) told the story of Nina, a Puerto Rican girl who struggles with the expectations her parents have for her to achieve the so-called American Dream. As these few examples reveal, Latinx teenagers are not invisible in mainstream U.S. culture. Rather, fictional teens such as *Spider-Man*'s Miles Morales, *I Am Not Your Perfect Mexican Daughter*'s Julia Reyes, *Party of Five*'s Acosta siblings, and *In the Heights*'s Nina Rosario comprise a growing body of pop-culture media that situates young Latinxs as three-dimensional individuals who have agency, authenticity, and bad-ass charisma.

*Latinx Teens: U.S. Popular Culture on the Page, Stage, and Screen* examines how Latinx teenagers influence twenty-first-century U.S. popular culture. Specifically, we explore the diverse ways that contemporary mainstream film, television, theatre, and young adult literature invoke, construct, and interpret adolescent Latinidad. The Latinx-ness of the fictional teens in this study speaks not only to how coming-of-age Latinx representation is performed in mainstream media, but also to how U.S. audiences consume Latinx characters and stories. Despite the roadblocks that the Latinx community faces in both real and fictional settings, Latinx teens in pop culture forge spaces that, as a result, institutionalize Latinidad. This growing body of work, while making Latinx adolescence mainstream, situates teen characters as both inside and outside of their Latinx communities and U.S. mainstream culture, conveying the complexities of assimilation, "fitting in," and refusing to "fit in" all at the same time.

We argue not only that Latinx teenagers contribute to U.S. popular culture but also that their identities and narratives offer a roadmap to understanding issues of representation, visibility, and the complexities of Latinidad, including racial politics that directly impact these communities. The cultural texts that we analyze exemplify how Latinx youth are (re)imagining U.S. popular culture by writing themselves into the narrative. By portraying real-life concerns, such as racialized immigration policies that were a hallmark of the Trump era from a specific adolescent perspective, seen in *Party of Five*, for example, contemporary U.S. popular culture representations of Latinx adolescence move beyond one-dimensional teen identities to examine issues that directly concern teen viewers. Although examining popular culture, this book draws upon and expands preliminary discussions we began in our edited volume, *Nerds, Goths, Geeks, and Freaks: Outsiders in Chicanx and Latinx Young Adult Literature* (University Press of Mississippi, 2020) to place Latinx adolescent storylines and voices front and center. By moving Latinx teen "weirdo" identities from the margins into the center, our book called not only for recognition of the multifaceted identities we have always known existed but also for an examination of Latinx young adult literature through the lens of the outsider, the queer, and the maligned. As we claimed in that book, we offer the position that privileging the representation of Latinx teenagers is the ideal lens through which to understand how power and representation in popular culture work.

## Why Latinx Teens?

*Latinx Teens: US Popular Culture on the Page, Stage, and Screen* explores the relationship between Latinx teenagers and U.S. popular culture in the first two decades of the twenty-first century. We pay particular attention to how the intersections of youth identity and coming of age materialize in various mainstream spaces, most notably film, television, young adult literature, and theatre. Our book investigates Latinx teen characters and narratives to reveal how young people are at the forefront of unravelling issues of race, ethnicity, gender, sexuality, class, and immigration. While *Latinx Teens* focuses on fictional representations across various pop-culture media, we acknowledge flesh-and-blood Latinx teens who navigate social, economic, racial, sexual, and geographic spaces in their daily lives. For example, in our television chapter's analysis of the fictional character Lucia Acosta of *Party of Five*, we discuss the significance of her burgeoning activism and how her storyline serves as an homage to real teen activists who have influenced present-day, ongoing resistance to white supremacy in law enforcement, immigration enforcement, and the educational curriculum. Although fictional, Lucia Acosta's experience is as real as it gets.

*Latinx Teens*'s primary concern is how and why Latinx teenagers influence both Latinx culture and U.S. pop culture. As we detail, young Latinxs have taken on a growing significance in recent decades as fictional pop-culture teens have begun to proliferate while Latinx youth across the United States have taken advantage of new digital media such as TikTok to insert themselves into the mainstream narrative. We thus acknowledge the power they have always had to manifest social change. By taking a multimodal interdisciplinary approach, we argue that contemporary portrayals of teenage Latinidad offer compelling identity narratives to better understand how Latinxs on the cusp of adulthood challenge, transform, expand, and reimagine not only Latinx identity, but, perhaps most significantly, its relationship to mainstream U.S. popular culture in the twenty-first century.

While there has been much recent scholarship on Latinx popular culture, most notably studies by Frederick Luis Aldama, Isabel Molina-Guzmán, Mary Beltrán, Tanya González and Eliza Rodríguez y Gibson, Arlene Dávila, Yeidy M. Rivero, and Jillian Báez, most extant scholarship pays little attention, if any, to the identities of Latinx teenagers. The seminal volume *The Routledge Companion to Latina/o Popular Culture* is one of the few collections that includes multiple chapters on media programming aimed at Latinx children, an area of scholarship that is vastly understudied. Departing from this foundational work, our book encompasses an analysis of popular culture primarily through the adolescent storyline. We believe that a discussion on Latinx popular culture centered specifically on Latinx teenagers is fundamental to our understanding of Latinx visibility on the page, stage, and screen. At present, there is no book-length study that focuses on Latinx teenagers in U.S. and Latinx popular culture. As such, our book makes a critical intervention into popular-culture studies, Latinx studies, education, and youth studies.

Rather than an overarching examination of Latinx representation in U.S. popular culture, this book takes at its core the position that, to study the relationship between Latinx identity and U.S. popular culture, we need to explore this with an eye on a group that is seldom portrayed as serious, deserving, or worthy of listening to: teenage Latinxs. By overlooking this demographic in studies of U.S. popular culture and Latinidad, we are missing the creative and critical ways that real-life Latinx adolescents are shaping up and shaking up their communities. Less about media constructions of Latinidad, the central focus of Mary Beltrán's *Latina/o Stars in U.S. Eyes*, for example, our work explores how fictional Latinx teen storylines offer creative and powerful renderings of what it means to be an adolescent in the twenty-first century. To better appreciate this, though, we do need to examine what these teens are up against, namely the dismal numbers regarding Latinx representation overall in the worlds of YA literature, film, drama, and television.

Perhaps the most prolific medium for Latinx teens has been literature. Despite the dismal statistics that Latinx authors and readers face, young adult literature has been one of the spaces that has consistently seen growth in Latinx novels and, subsequently, fully fledged Latinx teenagers on the page. According to a study by the University of Wisconsin's Cooperative Children's Book Center, just under 6 percent of young adult and children's books published in 2017 were written by Latinx authors (*Publishing Statistics*). Moreover, the gap in publishing stories about Latinx teens extends across the field, including the scholarship on Latinx literature in general. *The Cambridge Companion to Latina/o Literature* does not include a single chapter on Latinx young adult literature, for example. Moreover, as Frederick Luis Aldama recognizes, "The two-thousand-plus-page behemoth, *The Norton Anthology of Children's Literature* (2005), does not include one US Latino author" (10). The paucity of both young adult publishing and corresponding scholarship hints that Latinx teens don't regularly fill the pages of young adult literature. As work by award-winning authors such as Elizabeth Acevedo, Guadalupe García McCall, Matt De La Peña, Benjamin Alire Sáenz, Erika L. Sánchez, and Adam Silvera reveals, Latinx teens *do* exist in YA literature and, moreover, they regularly penetrate the mainstream.

In recent years, the small screen has become a common site to portray teenage Latinidades. In 2020 alone we witnessed new shows such as *The Expanding Universe of Ashley Garcia* (Netflix), *Diary of a Future President* (Disney+), *Party of Five* (Freeform), and *Love, Victor* (Hulu), not to mention new seasons of *On My Block* (Netflix, 2018–21) and *One Day at a Time* (Netflix/Pop TV, 2017–20). Although not primarily concerned with Latinx adolescence, the overwhelming popularity and appeal of Starz Channel's *Vida* (2018–20) and Netflix's *Gentefied* (2020–present) proved that Latinx communities are prime audiences. This sudden groundswell of new television content featuring Latinx teenagers has worked to push against the underrepresentation that young Latinxs have historically faced. While there have seemingly always been Latinx teens on the small screen, from *Welcome Back, Kotter* (1975–79) and *My So-called Life* (1995–94) to *Saved by the Bell* (1989–93) and *The Mickey Mouse Club* (1989–96), there has never been a moment for representation quite like the present. Where Latinx teens once faced stereotypical representation on television, TV shows in the twenty-first century situate Latinx youth as multidimensional characters. They are no longer sidekicks; their narratives are essential to the world of their TV show.

The lack of representation in film is no different. According to a 2019 study by USC Annenberg, only 3 percent of main characters in the top 100 grossing films from 2007–18 were Latinx. And, per usual, many of these roles waded in stereotypical waters. The study included over 1,200 films from the twenty-first century and emphatically revealed that Latinx characters were often portrayed as working class, uneducated, and/or criminals (Smith et al). That is, these Latinxs lacked any semblance of authentic Latinx culture, where films like *The Fast and the Furious* (2001) were the main mode of Latinx representation. And, to make matters worse, if you exclude films in which Cameron Diaz, Jennifer Lopez, and Jessica Alba played leading roles, then there is even more of a noticeable gap. Even so, to assume that the lack of representation corresponds to a lack of Latinx narratives on film would be incorrect. Films such as *Real Women Have*

*Curves* (2002), *Mosquita y Mari* (2012), *Girlfight* (2000), *Raising Victor Vargas* (2002), *Filly Brown* (2012), and *Spider-Man: Into the Spider-Verse* (2018) all feature three-dimensional depictions of Latinx teens coming of age.

Despite the Latinx community facing issues of representation in theatre, the twenty-first century has seen an explosion of sorts of Latinx theatre. The Broadway League's annual audience demographics report reveals that Latinx attendance grew by 61 percent from 2010 to 2018, demonstrating a growing interest on the part of Latinx theatregoers in the country's most legitimate stages (Broadway League). Yet just 3 percent of roles went to Latinx actors during the 2014–15 theatre season in New York City (AAPAC). The same report revealed that almost 90 percent of playwrights from 2016–17 were white men. Although it may be easy to dismiss these statistics as only germane to New York City, to do so would turn a blind eye to the tremendous influence that Broadway and Off-Broadway theatre have on theatre across the country. From 2010–20, Latinx theatre hit a second gear. Playwrights Karen Zacarías and Quiara Alegría Hudes are annually among the most-produced playwrights in the country. Advocacy groups such as the 50 Playwrights Project and Project Am I Right? have demonstrated that there is no shortage of Latinx theatre talent. The Latinx Theatre Commons has helped create a cohesive network of artists, advocates, and scholars who have leveraged their individual tools to create the nation's most formidable ethnic theatre movement. And, of course, the most famous piece of theatre in recent decades is *Hamilton* (2015), Lin-Manuel Miranda's Latinx remix of Alexander Hamilton's journey from poor immigrant from the Caribbean to one of the most powerful men in the newly founded United States. While Hamilton's son Phillip, originally played by Anthony Ramos, situates a Latino teen as central to the show's second act, he is but one example of how Latinx teens have become central to mainstream theatre across the country. Whether it is musicals such as *In the Heights* by Lin-Manuel Miranda and Quiara Alegría Hudes and *Miss You Like Hell* (2016) by Hudes and Erin McKeown or plays such as *Swimming While Drowning* (2016) by Emilio Rodriguez or *Our Dear Dead Drug Lord* (2019) by Alexis Scheer, Latinx dramatists have routinely turned to young people to theorize themes such as community, citizenship, queerness, and politics.

As these statistics convey, there is a gap in the representation of Latinx narratives across various popular culture media. By any measure, this data is alarming and demonstrates how it is impossible to argue that Latinidad is not underrepresented in U.S. popular culture. And it certainly does not correspond with the U.S.'s fastest-growing demographic, now comprising 17 percent of the population and soon to be the nation's largest ethnic group by 2045. Throughout this book, we do not harp on the lack of representation. Rather, we are committed to documenting the work that has been done in order to make Latinx teens more visible in popular culture. That said, there has been a notable increase in Latinx representation in the first two decades of the 2000s. And, not surprisingly, teen stories are at the forefront of this cultural movement. Latinx young adult literature regularly occupies the coveted *New York Times* Best Seller list. There are now enough television shows and films featuring Latinx teen protagonists to overwhelm even the most dedicated screen addict. In theatre, playwrights and composers Lin-Manuel Miranda, Quiara Alegría Hudes, and Karen Zacarías have become *the* mainstream. Accordingly, this cultural production has led to increased attention from students and educators. To understand teenage Latinidad is to understand contemporary U.S. culture. Latinx teens *are* U.S. American teens, and, therefore, their stories are crucial to understanding teenager identity and experience in the twenty-first century.

## Welcome to Latinx Teens 101

*Latinx Teens* is organized like a syllabus for a semester-long college course or a year-long high school course. That is, each chapter represents a unit focusing on a specific medium. We structured the book like a college syllabus because we envisioned a book that would be accessible for college courses in youth studies/Latinx studies/media studies, for eager-eyed first year students to seasoned seniors on the verge of graduation. We envision *Latinx Teens* as an anchor text, with professors filling out the syllabus with readings specific to their field, thus building out a well-rounded undergraduate course on Latinx youth. To guide researchers and students alike, each chapter concludes with a "For Further Reading" and "For Further Viewing" section filled with suggested creative and scholarly texts to continue learning. With this panoramic approach, we believe this book will appeal to undergraduates and established researchers alike. We selected the texts, films, plays, and television shows to reflect the heterogeneity of Latinx adolescence while also demonstrating the varying social and geographical spaces these young people occupy. Although not comprehensive, these texts provide an in-depth overview of the spectrum of Latinx teen identities in the first two decades of the twenty-first century.

Each chapter offers an overview in addition to a more detailed analysis of four notable novels, television shows, films, and plays that speak to themes that are indispensable to understanding Latinx youth identities and experiences fully. Each of the works in this book passes what Frederick Luis Aldama and Christopher Gonzalez dub the "Latinx Bechdel Test" in *Reel Latinxs: Representation in U.S. Film and TV*. Riffing off Alison Bechdel's Bechdel Test, which focuses on multifaceted female characters, the Latinx Bechdel Test requires that a film or television show, for example, has two named Latinx characters that have a conversation with each other about something other than an Anglo. As with the original Bechdel Test, even works of cultural production that would appear to overwhelmingly pass the test don't even come close. For example, despite Rickie Vasquez becoming a standout character on the 1990s TV series *My So-Called Life*, the show doesn't pass the Latinx Bechdel Test. The same can be said for *Welcome Back, Kotter* and *Napoleon Dynamite* (2004). This does not even include television shows such as *The Fresh Prince of Bel-Air* (1990–96) that featured Afro-Latinx actors Alfonso Ribeiro and Tatyana Ali in their roles as Carlton and Ashley Banks, which completely erased their Latinidad. With this in mind, *Latinx Teens* pays particular attention to works that *do* pass the Latinx Bechdel Test, as we believe these examples offer more opportunities to explore authentic and diverse representations of Latinidad.

While there is no shortage of texts examining Latinxs and media, seen in important texts such as Frederick Luis Aldama and Christopher Gonzalez's *Reel Latinxs: Representation in U.S. Film and TV*; Tanya Gonzalez and Eliza Rodriguez y Gibson's *Humor and Latina/o Camp in Ugly Betty: Funny Looking*; Isabel Molina-Guzmán's *Latinas and Latinos on TV*; *Contemporary Latina/o Media: Production, Circulation, Politics*, edited by Arlene Dávila and Yeidy M. Rivero; and

Jillian Baez's *In Search of Belonging: Latinas, Media, and Citizenship*, to name only a few, there is no book that looks at popular culture specifically through a representation of Latinx teenagers. This book serves as a critical intervention to insist that we must privilege the stories of Latinx teenagers in television, film, theatre, and literature to get to the heart of Latinx popular culture. As such, our book is influenced by the pathbreaking work of the aforementioned scholars by addressing the noticeable absence of Latinx teenagers from the discussion. This book is the first text that specifically examines Latinx adolescence in popular culture, exploring themes around representation, identity, gender, (in)visibility, sexuality, and race. Moreover, the works explored in *Latinx Teens* speak to the ethnic and racial spectrum of the Latinx community; as these representative examples reveal, there is neither a singular definition of Latinidad nor is there a single way to be Latinx.

*Latinx Teens* begins on the small screen. In the first chapter, "'I want you to know me. Who I really am': Latinx Teens on the Small Screen," we examine some of the most popular and most recent television shows featuring almost exclusively Latinx teenage casts: *Diary of a Future President*; *On My Block*; *Party of Five*; and *Love, Victor*. Exploring themes such as sexuality, coming out/coming into oneself as a queer Latinx teen, the racialized political landscape of the Trump era, and complicated family relationships, we discuss the distinct Latinx adolescent representation that has proliferated the small screen within the last five years. We provide a literature review/overview, citing major scholarship that has examined Latinx representation on television, which has seldom taken into account Latinx adolescent characters.

Chapter two, "'Do you want to be a papi chulo or a papi feo?': Latinx Teens on the Big Screen," shifts from the small screen to the silver screen. We explore how filmmakers have taken to the big screen to expand notions of Latinx teenage identities and experiences over the past two decades. In addition to providing an overview of Latinx teenagers in contemporary film, we focus on four films: *Real Women Have Curves*, *Raising Victor Vargas*, *Mosquita y Mari*, and *Spider-Man: Into the Spider-Verse*. The Latinx teenage leads in these films offer fertile ground to examine themes such as feminist coming-to-consciousness, friendship and queerness, masculinity, and the reality of Afro-Latinx superheroes.

Chapter three, "'I Sign Myself Across the Line': Latinx Teens on the Page," begins with an overview of the field of Latinx YA literature to identify key scholarly interventions. Specifically, we focus on novels by major writers who are at the very top of Latinx YA literature: *Juliet Takes a Breath* by Gabby Rivera, *The Poet X* by Elizabeth Acevedo, *Aristotle and Dante Discover the Secrets of the Universe* by Benjamin Alire Sáenz, and *They Both Die at the End* by Adam Silvera. These novels explore the breadth and complexity of, among other issues, Afro-Latinx identity, queerness, coming of age/coming out, and family relationships.

In chapter four, "'I'm only nineteen but my mind is older': Latinx Teens on Stage," we move from the page to the stage to engage with contemporary Latinx theatre. We begin our theatrical journey with the most famous piece of theatre of the twenty-first century—Lin-Manuel Miranda's 2015 Broadway musical *Hamilton*. Focusing on Alexander Hamilton's son, Phillip, a Latino teen as seen in the musical, offers the reader an entry point into how Latinx teenagers have penetrated contemporary mainstream theatre. From there, the chapter includes a survey of the field before focusing more in depth on four case studies—*In the Heights* by Lin-Manuel Miranda and Quiara Alegría Hudes, *Swimming While Drowning* by Emilio Rodriguez, *Our Dear Dead Drug Lord* by Alexis Scheer, and *I Am Not Your Perfect Mexican Daughter* by Isaac Gómez, adapted from Erika L. Sánchez's best-selling novel. These four pieces of theatre include important themes to understand teenagers, most notably how young Latinxs inherit generational expectations from their parents, how queerness and homelessness intersect, how teenage girls get to be bad and push against their parents' conservative views, and how writing can be used as a tool to heal.

*Latinx Teens*'s conclusion, "Shaking Up the World: Latinx Teen Activists," pivots from fictional Latinx teens seen across various popular culture media to real-life Latinx teenage activists who have made use of social media in recent years to further complicate Latinidad. Specifically, we focus on Emma González, Ramon Contreras, Sage Grace Dolan-Sandrino, and Latinx TikTokers. By using platforms such as Instagram, Twitter, and TikTok, these young people leverage digital networks as activist platforms and, as a result, extend the possibilities of what it means to be a Latinx teenager in the twenty-first century.

We insist that readers, scholars, and students see Latinx teen activists as "game changers" who use social media presence to advocate for significant social change, such as gun-control legislation and transgender rights.

*¡Adelante!*

We wrote the bulk of this book in the early and latter months of 2020 during a particularly somber moment in history. While the COVID-19 pandemic raged on, we found ourselves with a deadline to fulfill amid the rapid transition to virtual teaching, virtual meetings, virtual everything. Zoom fatigue, hopelessness, and exhaustion were just some of what we were feeling. The stress and anxiety we experienced as teachers and as human beings, however, was temporarily assuaged by writing this book and by spending hours and hours of time on our living room couches screening, reading, and texting each other our impressions and ideas. We were inspired by the prospect of a Latina commander in chief and heartbroken by the inhumane deportation of parents that reduced a family to a party of five rather than a party of seven. Young adult literature, theatre, and film kept us grounded, entertained, and excited all at the same time. Celebrating the highs, lows, and gray areas in between, these Latinx teens picked us up and propelled us to write this book that is now in your hands. It's safe to say that Latinx teens saved us. Were it not for these teenagers who fueled our creative spirit, this period would have been all the more devastating for us. It is our hope that this little book of ours will inspire you as well, readers. Now let's get started!

1

# "I WANT YOU TO KNOW ME. WHO I REALLY AM"

## Latinx Teens on the Small Screen

When Fox's musical series *Glee* (2009–15) debuted, audiences were immediately thrown into the musical world of New Directions, a glee club filled with teens on the margins at their high school. One of those teens was Santana Lopez (played by Afro-Latina actor Naya Rivera), a bad-girl cheerleader who joins New Directions as a spy but soon falls in love with the club. According to Erika Abad, an expert in Latinx youth representation on television, "As a queer Latina over the majority of her character's storyline, Rivera's Santana Lopez developed into a complex person in ways that had begun to break away from the sexual spitfire stereotype that was written onto her character within the first seasons of the show" ("Revisiting"). Throughout the course of the series, audiences learn that Santana's tough-girl attitude was a mask she wore as she struggled to come to terms with her attraction to girls. Santana's coming-of-age story reached a peak in the November 29, 2011 episode, "I Kissed a Girl," which specifically tackles Santana's coming to terms with her queerness. No longer okay with living a lie, she decides to come out to her family. Her parents are accepting, but, when she comes out to her grandmother, she finds anything but acceptance. In one of the series' most touching scenes, Santana sits down with her grandmother at the kitchen table and reveals: "I love girls the way that I'm supposed to feel about boys. It's just something that's always been inside of me. And I really want to share it with you because I love you so much. I want you to know me. Who I really am." Santana's grandmother responds by telling her it's a sin, calling her a sin *vergüenza*, and disowning her. Eventually, her grandmother comes around, and the two repair their relationship.

Nearly nine years later, the power of not just this scene but of Santana Lopez as a queer Latina teen on one of the most popular television series of all time was still palpable. On July 8, 2020, Naya Rivera died in a tragic drowning incident at Lake Piru, California. As has become common, Gleeks, or *Glee* fans, took to social media to celebrate Rivera's life and to share how her embodiment as a queer Latina teen was transformative to their own lives. Many Twitter users shared their favorite Naya Rivera scenes and wrote brief eulogies about how Santana impacted their coming-of-age experiences. On Twitter, @finelinelesbian wrote, "THIS was the scene that changed my life. Naya made it feel so real & genuine. I used to watch this on repeat as a young closeted lesbian so that I would feel less alone. I knew that if I came out, I would be disowned/kicked out." Afro-Latina writer Carmen Phillips tweeted, "I know this: Naya Rivera fought like hell for Santana Lopez's coming out story. And seeing an Afro-Latina come out to her Abuela gave me the courage to do the same. And coming out literally changed everything in my life." Writer Alejandro Heredia tweeted, "Naya Rivera's Santana was the first time I saw a queer Black Latinx person represented on any medium of art. She didn't have to be respectable, kind, loving, anything but who she was. For a queer Dominican kid growing up in The Bronx, that was liberating." Other Gleeks on Twitter revealed how this scene resonated with them as high schoolers, instilling confidence in some closeted queer teens to come out to their families, even giving some of them the exact words to do so.

While we can lay down the numbers on Latinx TV viewership and the stats on Latinx shows and characters on the small screen, there are no numbers that can truly encompass *how* representation on television affects actual Latinx teenagers. Instead, we must rely on firsthand accounts of what it means for a Latinx teen who is coming-of-age to bear witness to another Latinx teen going through the same struggles of identity and belonging. As Naya Rivera's work on *Glee* attests, there is power in representation, and, to put it lightly, Latinx teens are hungry to see their stories on television. This profound moment in TV history reveals the powerful, affirming, and validating experience of witnessing legitimate storylines that capture what it means to be a queer Latinx teen.

Despite Latinxs comprising the United States' largest ethnic group, "Latina/o characters are almost invisible, and when they are visible it is in mostly stereotyped ways" (Molina-Guzman 17). Although this is certainly true today, the teen characters in this chapter all push against stereotypes. The four television shows we discuss in this chapter—*Diary of a Future President* (2020–); *On My Block* (2018–21); *Party of Five* (2020); and *Love, Victor* (2020–)—are significant for how they privilege the voices and experiences of fictional Latinx teens in ways that real-life teens can relate to. Whether it's hesitation to come out as queer because you're afraid of your parents' rejection or trying to live a "normal" high school life when the only country you've ever known has decided to deport your parents, these shows present Latinx teenagers in highly nuanced ways that depart from the simplistic sidekick role. Rather than portray Latinx youth as "vulnerable" and "victims" of negative media attention, as they are perceived by their families (Baez 121), these teens are much more multidimensional in their quest for agency. Departing from Baez's important work that documents Latinx, particularly Latina, engagement with media as audience members (5), this chapter foregrounds representation of Latinx teens to probe narratives of belonging, identity development, queerness, and other thematic concerns. While the protagonist of *Diary of a Future President* is not yet a teenager, we have chosen to include this series because of how it deftly captures what it's like to be on the cusp of adolescence, which is fundamental to understanding the teenage experience. Moreover, in this chapter, we exclusively focus on English-language television. Although the Spanish language is generally attributed to the Latinx population, the numbers tell us that fewer and fewer Latinx teens are fully bilingual. We could certainly expand this book to include Spanish-language media and Latinx teenagers' role in shaping that dynamic, but we have selected English to represent the reality that it is the primary language among this generation of young people. Regardless of language, though, we believe Latinx teens are having a moment in television, and this chapter explores what this means, why it matters, and why there is still much more work to be done.

# "... still only a blip on the representational radar": Latinxs on TV

As the 1990s came to a close, the four major broadcast networks (ABC, CBS, Fox, and NBC) released a slate of twenty-six new television series in 1999. Not a single one of these shows featured a Latinx leading character (none featured a Black or Asian American lead, for that matter). The quotation that begins this chapter section is, unfortunately, apt, as the authors of those words, Frederick Luis Aldama and Christopher Gonzalez, tell us: "The Latinx demographic numbers are more than abundant, yet we're still only a blip on the representational radar" (*Reel Latinxs* 29). Twenty years later, not much has changed on network television. With the cancellation of ABC's *The Beauty and the Baker* (2020) after one season of middling results during the COVID-19 pandemic, broadcast television was once again without a show dedicated to the lives and realities of the Latinx community. Even though there are many instances of Latinx lead characters on major broadcast television, none of these shows is exclusively about Latinxs. While Latinxs made undeniable gains in representation in nearly every space over the first two decades of the twenty-first century, the gaps on television's four major networks are glaring. But they don't reveal the whole story. As technology has advanced, so have digital streaming capabilities. The rise and success of streaming platforms such as Netflix, Hulu, Amazon Prime, and Disney+ would have been unthinkable in 1999, but in 2020 they are the norm, and, in many cases, they set the tone in the TV industry. In fact, we are in what television studies scholar Amanda Lotz calls TV's "post-network era," and, as a result, the possibilities are endless. Coincidentally, the post-network era has enabled what media studies scholar Isabel Molina-Guzmán refers to as the "post-racial era of U.S.-produced television," which "celebrates the visibility of ethnic-racial difference and moves away from stereotypes" (5). Indeed, the case studies that follow in this chapter would be unthinkable even twenty years ago.

A 2016 study by the Media, Diversity and Social Change Initiative at the University of Southern California's Annenberg School for Communication and Journalism revealed that just 5.8% of named characters on broadcast, cable, and streaming outlets were Latinx (Smith et al). Notably, this sparse number is actually an improvement from recent years, with around 2–3% of television roles being Latinx during the 2012–13 season. Compared to the Latinx community being over 55 million strong and comprising roughly 17% of the U.S. population, these numbers are jarring even if they do point to an upward tick in representation.

On average, there are around 500 scripted TV shows per year. Not surprisingly, when Latinx characters do appear in television, they often traffic in tired stereotypes of Latinxs. Cardboard characters such as maids, drug dealers, gang members, and petty criminals fill the TV screen even today and play into former president Donald Trump's hate-speech rhetoric that "When Mexico sends its people, they're not sending the best. They're sending people that have lots of problems and they're bringing those problems" (Qtd. in Ye Hee Lee). While this June 2015 quote is from the beginning of Trump's initial presidential campaign, his words portended what was to come during his presidency. These stereotypes don't give teens positive examples to follow. As Rocío Rivadeneyra, who studies adolescent exposure to media, explains it, "Television is an important influence on youth, shaping their knowledge, beliefs, attitudes, and behavior" (394). It is no secret that we shape our identities not just from those around us but also from the media that we are exposed to. Negative portrayals, therefore, may affect self-esteem. As television is such a popular form of entertainment, positioning multifaceted Latinx stories on the small screen directly pushes against the ways that the mainstream has historically sought to paint Latinidad with a broad stroke and, as a result, render the Latinx community invisible. Yet, as contemporary TV makers demonstrate, there has been a wealth of Latinx representation on television, especially in the last decade and, in particular, after Donald Trump took office in 2017.

Of course, there have always been Latinx characters on television. Classic shows such as *Welcome Back, Kotter* (1975–79); *Saved by the Bell* (1989–93); *My So-Called Life* (1994–95); and *Qué Pasa, USA?* (1977–80) all portrayed Latinidad with varying success. And, of course, Latinx actors have often found work even if their ethnic identity was erased. Shows such as *The Fresh Prince of Bel-Air* (1990–96) featured Afro-Latinx actors Alfonso Ribeiro and Tatyana Ali as Carlton and Ashley Banks in roles that completely eliminated their Latinidad. As the 1990s came to a close, the popular Fox sitcom *That '70s Show*, which aired from 1998–2006, appeared set to update the narrative about Latinx teens. *That '70s Show* followed a group of teens in 1970s Wisconsin, one of whom was Fez, played by Wilmer Valderrama. Born in Miami to Colombian and Venezuelan parents, Fez was used as comic relief as he routinely struggled to learn how to be a U.S. teen. That is, he learns how to be white, just like his friends. His Latinidad, therefore, is often the butt of the joke. His friends make fun of his accent and frequently try to guess where he is from. While television shows such as *That '70s Show* did do important, if not problematic, work to position Latinx characters away from harmful stereotypes, ultimately many of these portrayals fall short. That said, they did pave the way for an increase in Latinidad on TV.

From 2000–20, there has been a marked increase in nuanced portrayals of Latinx teenagers on television. This harkens back to television's history of targeting teenagers as an audience. Television marketed to teenagers, what television and media scholar Stefania Marghitu calls "teen tv," "adhere[s] to elements of the coming-of-age story . . . the protagonist feels alienated from the adult world she is on the threshold of entering. This conflict is intertwined with a passionate story of first love and new discoveries during the transition from child to adult." From *George Lopez* (2002–07), depicting a middle-class Latinx family, to Hulu's *East Los High*'s Latinx high schoolers in East Los Angeles from 2013–17, there have been enough Latinx teens on the small screen to fill their own book. Although stereotypes remain an issue, teens in the twenty-first century offer more nuanced representations of Latinidad than in the past. Notable examples include the following shows: For two seasons from 2001–02, Nickelodeon's *Taina* gave us teen phenom Taina, who aspires to be an actor and singer. Her quest for stardom drives much of the plot as she navigates the halls of Manhattan High School of the Performing Arts. Every episode highlighted her daydreams of stardom, and oftentimes episodes culminated with Taina performing a song. The Disney Channel's *Wizards of Waverly Place* (2007–12) is notable for launching the career of Selena Gomez, who played one of the show's wizard trio. *Elena of Avalor* (Disney Channel/Disney Junior, 2016–18) follows teen princess Elena Castillo Flores, who has saved her kingdom from an evil sorceress and now must rule her kingdom at the age of sixteen. And, in 2019, Netflix debuted *Mr. Iglesias*, complete with a host of teens who have Gabriel Iglesias as their teacher; Mr. Iglesias helps these gifted misfit high schoolers reach their full potential throughout the series. However, as we were writing this chapter, the 2020 Emmy Nominations were released, and, despite the explosion of series featuring Latinx teen storylines, none of these was nominated for award categories. This speaks to the larger issue of invisibility of Latinx teenagers in the media and the more pertinent issue we consider throughout this book: why popular culture that centers Latinx adolescence is not treated with the seriousness it deserves.

That said, there has been one overarching theme on television in recent decades—Latinx nerds. The small screen has always been filled with white boy geniuses. Shows such as *Doogie Howser, M.D.* (1989–93) and *Young Sheldon* (2017–) both feature very smart white boys, and, although these shows don't always focus on teenagers, they leave little room for Latinx teens to be Brown and nerdy. Aside from *Modern Family* (2009–20), which features Colombian American uber nerd and hopeless romantic Manny Delgado-Pritchett (played by Rico Rodriguez), intellectual Latinx teens are rarely depicted in major network successes. Writing for the *Los Angeles Times*, Monica Castillo declared that the Latina genius had finally cemented her place alongside other archetypes on the small screen. Intellectual teenage Latinas are playing significant roles in Disney+ and Netflix series such as *One Day at a Time* (2017–), *On My Block* (2018–21), *Never Have I Ever* (2020–), *Diary of a Future President* (2020–), *Party of Five* (2020), and *The Expanding Universe of Ashley Garcia* (2020–) (and let's not forget *Ugly Betty* and *Jane the Virgin*, both of which paved the way for these LatiNerds). Considering that, according to Molina-Guzmán, Latinas are "the most likely of all ethnic and racial groups to be depicted in sexualized attire, partially nude, or as the object of heterosexual attraction," it is especially significant that Latina nerds have entered the fray in such a pronounced way (17). Latina nerds on TV, even as they may express interest in "typical" adolescent pastimes like dating and makeup, do so not at the expense of their nerdiness. Moreover, this nerdiness is intrinsically part of their expression of Latina adolescence; being a nerd *is* Latina.

The Latina nerd trope even goes back a little further with Freeform's *The Fosters* (2013–18), which portrays the mixed-race family of lesbian couple Stef and Lena's biological and adopted children. Among the four adopted children are Latinx twins Jesus and Mariana Adams Foster. Jesus is a wrestling phenom, but Mariana is an intellectual. Fabiola Torres (*Never Have I Ever*) is a queer Afro-Latina whose main hobby is robotics and whose definition of dressing "sexy" to school is to wear a boy's polo shirt. *One Day at a Time* features Elena Alvarez, an A+ student, champion debater, and outspoken activist. And, as her show's title character, Ashley Garcia gets the most real estate to get Brown and nerdy. Garcia is a fifteen-year-old Mexican American wonder who already has a PhD and works at the Jet Propulsion Laboratory in Pasadena, California. Her life is filled with success after success, but there is one glaring absence—she has forgotten what it's like to be a teenager. She doesn't know how to hang out with people her age or how to deal with crushes on boys.

Television shows such as *Never Have I Ever* and *The Expanding Universe of Ashley Garcia* convey how, despite how much these Latina nerds have it all figured out (just like the teenage characters we discuss in the remainder of this chapter), they are still in the thick of their coming-of-age experiences, and, that being so, they have room to grow and endure the highs and lows of being a teenager.

### Cuban American Girlhood and Eventual Commander in Chief: *Diary of a Future President*

When we think of streaming channels like Disney+, our immediate reaction might be to reduce its significance. It's a channel used by exhausted, overworked parents to entertain their children, we might think. It's a kids' channel, nothing more. And while that may be true, what does it say that, while researching for this book, we, nerdy academics of a certain age, couldn't stop raving about a young Cubanita character named Elena Cañero-Reed (played by Tess Romero), a precocious, serious, politically minded twelve-year-old who dreams of one day being president of the United States? The appeal of *Diary of a Future President* (2020), created by Ilana Peña, cannot be overlooked, drawing its viewers in, adults and children alike, because of its seldom-seen serious treatment of a tween girl of color. Elena's aspirations, which she chronicles daily in her journal, are treated with the seriousness and care they deserve. She is treated as a human being who is worthy of respect and care, whose opinions matter.

Although Elena is technically not yet a teenager, the show is invested in how she navigates adolescence and longs to be a teenager. Being a fully-fledged teen, in Elena's eyes, is to have it all figured out—school, family, boys—you name it. Throughout the first season, we sit on pins and needles with Elena as she waits for her first period. When she finally begins menstruating, she tells us, "It seems like my childhood was in the rearview mirror." Her mother, Gabi, throws her a feast to celebrate her womanhood. As the mother and daughter duo eat comfort food like greasy pizza, hamburgers, and fries, we might as well be celebrating from our sofas at home. This highly significant moment is precisely why we knew we needed to discuss *Diary* in this book. Elena's not quite a tween, but she's getting there, and this episode in particular foreshadows what the beginning of menstruation will lead to: growing up, maturity, and the unknown that is young womanhood. The show depicts the anticipation of becoming a teenager and enjoying all of the benefits that accompany it. She will be taken more seriously, come into her own, and find out who she is.

While *Love, Victor*'s Latinidad, for example, is at best generic and wades into stereotypical waters regarding gender and sexuality (more on that later in the chapter), Elena's Cubanness is evident at every turn. *Diary* asserts and embraces her Cuban identity. She asks her mother about what it was like to arrive from Cuba, wants to learn more about this history, and genuinely shows curiosity about this aspect of her family. Her mother, Gabi, makes Cuban tostadas and cafecito for breakfast; she burns her hand and yells in Spanish. And, in one of the show's best storylines, her brother Bobby struggles with the "ñ" in their last name, feeling shame and embarrassment that it "looks like a worm" before realizing that the "ñ" is part of what makes him special. Bobby learns something that Elena already knows—he should be proud to be Cuban American and not be afraid of correcting people, even teachers, who anglicize his name.

*Diary of a Future President* begins on Elena Cañero-Reed's first day as president of the United States. Played in the future by Gina Rodriguez, who also produces the show, President Elena's White House is the antithesis to the real-life one at the time of the show's debut in 2020. Whereas the Trump administration was a bastion of whiteness, Cañero-Reed's White House is filled with people of color, many of them women. As the nation's first Latina POTUS, all eyes are on her. Will she royally mess up? Will she "prove" that Latinas have no business serving as commander in chief? It's her first day, and, to help combat her nerves, she opens an unexpected package from her mother—her forgotten middle-school diary, which will serve her as she tackles her new role as Leader of the Free World. Indeed, every great leader was once a middle schooler. Middle school is messy and universal; we've all lived through it—even future commanders in chief. With Elena's present and future set, the show transitions to the past to tell the story of how a Cuban American girl grew up to be the most powerful person in the United States. We know her future, but we need to learn what it took for a Latina to become the POTUS. Elena's coming-of-age experience details the challenges of growing up Latina. As she finds success and taps into her ability to achieve greatness, Elena's journey is uniquely positioned on Disney+ to inspire young girls to be fearless, not unlike Netflix's *The Baby-Sitters Club* (2020–). *Diary of a Future President* conveys the importance of nerdy young Latinas having the opportunity to watch television with characters who look and act like them.

Each episode title riffs on Elena's future job as president, demonstrating the parallels between her teenage and adult selves. While adult Elena may engage in "Disaster Relief" after a hurricane wrecks the Gulf Coast, young Elena uses the same blueprint to navigate the mean girls and the politics of middle-school friendships. Throughout season one, Elena asks herself what her raison d'etre is—what is her reason for being alive? In episode three, she wonders if her raison d'etre is hurricane preparation and relief. She runs against Ryan, a white bro, for Orange Bay Middle School's Hurricane Watch Captain. As with everything else, Elena takes her campaign seriously, giving an impassioned speech about family. Elena has a plan for everything, and her post as Hurricane Watch Captain will only portend the way she will eventually respond to real-life catastrophes such as Hurricane Katrina or Maria. Following her rousing speech, Ryan tells his classmates that, simply put, a hurricane means there won't be football. Ryan, of course, gets more applause. Elena's loss stings at first, but she learns an important life lesson. She thought she had to have everything figured out and know what her purpose in life was, even at twelve years old. Elena reflects, "But there's no rush to figure it out because if it really does matter, you'll figure it out eventually." This is what the show does best. In every episode, Elena learns something new, be it from her mother or a friend, but the series does so in a way that honors young people's ambitions while teaching them a thing or two about how to achieve these goals without shaming them for messing up along the way. Elena isn't perfect, and that's precisely what makes her relatable, funny, and cool as hell.

Season one ends with the most exciting part of sixth grade—the class trip to the Florida State Capitol in Tallahassee. The trip proves transformational for Elena. She pushes against the exclusivity of middle-school mean girls and popular cliques by throwing an inclusive class party in her hotel room. Whereas her "friend" Jessica's initial party idea was to be a super exclusive party reserved for only the cool kids, Elena changes the narrative and decides to throw her own party where everyone is welcome. There is space for every type of student in Elena's "tent"—cool kids, quiet kids, loud kids, unpopular kids, weird kids, and the like. While this episode speaks to Elena's budding political consciousness, it's not even the most meaningful part of her time in Tallahassee. During her visit to the state capitol, she listens to State Senator Morales address the class. Later, Elena runs into Senator Morales in the bathroom, and when Elena asks her to sign an autograph, the senator offers up some words of wisdom to her young future political colleague, reminding this up-and-comer to be herself and not to sacrifice authenticity for a few popularity points. Just as Alexandria Ocasio-Cortez inspires young Latinxs from her position in the United States House of Representatives, the fictional Morales inspires young Elenita to "keep calm and carry on," because Elena is exactly the kind of future AOC we all need.

In addition to Elena's characterization, *Diary of a Future President* is fully invested in pushing against stereotypes of gendered Latinidad. For example, Elena's mother, Gabriela Cañero-Reed, is a highly educated lawyer. With few exceptions, professional Latinas are almost never visible as television characters. Gabi loves her two children, Bobby and Elena, and even as she holds authority over them as a parent, she does not dismiss their legitimate emotions and actions, instead encouraging them to vocalize their fears, anger, and frustrations. When Bobby struggles to articulate his conflicted feelings of attraction toward another boy, his friend, the series treats this moment with tenderness *and* humor. Bobby can only explain his feelings through a

"I want you to know me. Who I really am"

27

reference to a computer game he plays, and when he asks Gabriela if she understands the game element he's talking about, she gently but humorously answers, "of course not, mi amor." Bobby does not share the extent of his budding queerness, leaving a cliffhanger for season two, but this compassionate, lighthearted moment is powerful in its treatment of a queer Latinx teen boy and his mother who loves him.

## Urban Latinx Adolescence and Friendship: *On My Block*

When *Stranger Things* debuted on Netflix in July 2016, it completely changed the name of the game for teenage representation on the small screen. The enormously popular series about a group of five teens navigating growing up while fighting off some pretty wild sci-fi monsters positioned the teenage experience as one of television's most discussed topics. Building off this momentum, Netflix has become *the* definitive streaming network for content by and for teens. The post-*Stranger Things* era of Netflix is, to be frank, obsessed with teens. The wave that *Stranger Things* created led to popular titles such as *13 Reasons Why* (2017–20), *To All the Boys I Loved Before* (2018), *The Kissing Booth* (2018), *Everything Sucks!* (2018), *End of the F\*\*\*ing World* (2017–19), and *Teenager Bounty Hunters* (2020). Yet, despite the successes of the aforementioned shows, none has been able to capture the attention of teens quite like *On My Block* (2018–21), one of the few examples of Netflix shows that actually centers Latinx teens.

Notably, *On My Block* was created to push against the pervasive whiteness of popular culture focused on young adults. According to creator Lauren Iungerich,

> And just thinking about all the shows that are currently on a lot of channels and the iconic shows about teen years... they're mostly through a white prism. Now, we're getting to see these kids from a different slice of life and we get to see representation of their experience, which is not a bleak and negative experience. (Yandoli)

The way that Iungerich and fellow creators Eddie Gonzalez and Jeremy Haft do this is simple. *On My Block* follows a group of four friends—Cesar, Jamal, Monse, and Ruby—growing up in South Central Los Angeles where gang violence is every bit a part of their reality as doing homework and going to school. This cohort of Black and Brown teens is living their best teenage years despite the constant threat of violence that is largely out of their control. Oh, and, of course, everything happens "on their block." Similar to films such as *Boyz n the Hood* (1991) and *Dope* (2015), *On My Block* questions how teens work within and against gang life to persevere in high school. *Degrassi* this is *not*.

The show's four protagonists are on the cusp of high school. They have the normal anxieties of high school mixed with the realities of living in a neighborhood in which gang life and the corresponding violence are the norm. Afro-Latina Monse Finnie (Sierra Capri) is an aspiring writer and budding feminist; she is excited about becoming a woman but must deal with the new way that the men around her see her. Ruby Martinez (Jason Genao) is smart and offers much comedic relief; his fast-talking ways prove successful for the group. Jamal Turner (Brett Gray) is the group's resident nerd; he's supposed to be a great athlete like his father, but he'd rather go on a *Goonies*-style treasure hunt than play football. And, finally, Cesar Diaz (Diego Tinoco) is trapped in his family's legacy of gang life. While each teen has their own journey, much of season one revolves around Cesar's struggles with gang life. Cesar's joining the gang disrupts the group's equilibrium. Even so, he doesn't have a choice. As he tells them, it's his "destiny"—"It's all I've got."

The show begins during the group's last summer before high school. They are at a 90s-looking party; teens are drinking, smoking, and dancing, and there isn't an adult in sight. Then it cuts to our four protagonists peeking from behind a fence. They are on the outside looking in, fully ready to be taken seriously and to be invited to the party. As freshmen, they are in the thick of their teenage years, on the brink of adulthood. Cesar declares, "*This* is about to be us. *This* is high school." Their dream is cut short when gunshots are heard, and the party quickly disbands, foreshadowing things to come. As the group runs down the street, they try to guess the caliber of the bullet. "That was a .38." "No, it sounded like a .45." After the final gunshot, they all say in unison, ".357" as they continue running down the street giggling. They joke about the gunshots because, quite frankly, hearing gunshots is a normal part of their lives, and, as tragic as it is, their strategy for survival is to make light of it and reduce any potential fear they may harbor.

Safely back at Ruby's house, his brother Mario gives them a piece of sage advice: "Don't go into high school without backup. You guys have to stick together to survive." The series then jumps to the beginning of freshman year of high school, and the central premise of the series begins to unfold—the highs and lows of friendship. At every turn, their friendship is tested. In the end, what they need most is each other.

Later, when Monse returns from summer writing camp, she learns that Cesar was jumped into Los Santos, the gang run by his brother, Oscar, who unexpectedly was released early from prison. Whether he liked it or not, he didn't have a choice. Cesar had to survive, and, on his block, surviving is joining Los Santos. Monse also learns that Cesar started a rumor about them to impress Oscar. By telling Los Santos that he hooked up with Monse, he "claims" her, which offers her protection from the gang, something that she explicitly tells Cesar that she doesn't need. She can protect herself. Even so, Monse is fiercely loyal to her friends and, accordingly, tells Ruby and Jamal that they have to save Cesar. They have no choice. Of course, none of their plans work, and they are forced to accept that this is Cesar's new reality whether he likes it or not.

What is more, death is a possibility in their community. In the third episode, someone brings a gun to the school dance, and it's abruptly cancelled. They shrug it off. This is their normal. Later in season one, the possibility of death remains prevalent. After Cesar gets in a fight with Latrelle, a former classmate who joined the rival gang, Oscar tells Cesar that he has to go into hiding or kill Latrelle. Under pressure, Cesar pulls a gun on Latrelle but tells him to flee, making him promise never to return. He then tells Oscar that he killed him. Latrelle, of course, shows up later because, well, being a teen isn't *that* easy, and Cesar will have to deal with his mistake.

In the season one finale, we have arrived at Ruby's "cousin" Olivia's quinceañera, which Ruby has been planning. The event is extravagant. Yet, this dream quince is interrupted by Latrelle, who shows up and tries to shoot Cesar but accidentally hits Ruby and Olivia instead. Ruby had finally just gotten his first kiss from Olivia; minutes later he is fighting for his life. Ruby survives, but Olivia, unfortunately, does not.

As these highs and lows of season one demonstrate, *On My Block* privileges peer relationships as an instrumental component of coming-of-age. They are each other's teachers. It's not the adults in their lives who are the sources of wisdom. Rather, it is each other. Friendship is a bedrock of the coming-of-age experience. As generations of parents have come to realize, who we hang with during our formative years can have a big impact on our identity and trajectory. During the teen years, there is a growing concern regarding acceptance and rejection. Young adults are worried about how they will be perceived for perhaps the first time. That being so, friendship is powerful and holds the potential to resemble the type of attachment that children have with their parents. According to developmental psychologist Jaana Juvonen, "even if that particular relationship doesn't last, it has ramifications on subsequent relationships" (Qtd. in Denworth). That is, teens are learning *how* to be friends and what their places are in their friend groups.

One thing is certain, *On My Block* is enormously popular with teens today. So-called Zoomers—that is, members of Generation Z—love *On My Block*. This reality was immediately evident when Trevor began teaching at Bellaire High School in 2018. His students continually told him that he *had* to watch the show (it was truly a demand, not a recommendation). When he asked them why they loved it, they all pointed to the show's relevance to the lives of actual teens of color and how the series depicts the importance of friendship as teens navigate the high school experience. One student said, "The bond the kids have together and their loyalty to one another." As another student put it, "they're ride or die friends." Others pointed to the show's realistic portrayals of teens of color: "It's juicy! Although the plot is dramatic, it still captures parts of the true teenage experience"; "it shows that living in a 'bad area' isn't always easy but having a group of friends changes everything"; "relates to teens growing up in real-life situations and shows us how to keep pushing." And another student pointed to the show's representation of Latinx teens: "I like that it is an urban show that just doesn't center around the Black community, but also focuses on Latinx teens."

Indeed, as the Latinx community continues to grow, it is imperative that television address this growing teenage demographic. And, by engaging with Latinx teenagerdom, TV must show the good with the bad, the beauty with the ugly. Whereas some shows may paint a rosy picture of growing up Latinx, which, of course, is many people's experience, teens of color need shows such as *On My Block* that will help them work through the rough parts. There are highs and lows of growing up Latinx, and *On My Block*, while offering a diversity of teenage experiences, conveys that one thing is critical to survival—friendship.

## Family Separation and Latinx Adolescence in the Trump Era: *Party of Five*

In 1994, a different kind of dramatic series premiered on the Fox network, this one revolving around the five Salinger siblings who are suddenly orphaned when their parents die in a tragic car accident. What was true then is true now: it's rare when dramatic television shows center the storylines around teenagers in a compassionate, critical way like *Party of Five*. But this one did, and it's no wonder that it was extremely popular with young viewers and remains a cult classic even now, decades later.

Fast forward to January 2020, when the cable channel Freeform announced a reboot of *Party of Five*. The original creators, Amy Lippman and Christopher Keyser, maintained virtually the same storyline—five siblings left alone to care for one another when their parents are suddenly absent. In a stunningly current twist, the creators rebranded the series from its original counterpart by telling a story that in many ways could only be told in 2020. Unlike the Salinger kids, whose parents die in a horrible accident, the Acosta siblings—Emilio, Beto, Lucia, Valentina, and baby Rafael—watch as their undocumented Mexican parents are deported right before their very eyes. In this sharp departure from its antecedent, 2020's reboot blurs the line between fact and fiction, representing the real terror Latinx communities felt when Donald Trump was sworn in as the forty-fifth president of the United States. To be sure, deportations were hardly unique to the Trump administration, given that President Barack Obama's two terms oversaw a record number of deportations. But something changed with Trump, and shows like *Party of Five* represent this shift in the public sphere, where overt, vocal displays of white supremacy get a pass. This fact is not surprising, considering Trump built almost his entire campaign platform on a "tough," no-holds-barred stance on immigration. Chants of "build the wall!" were a staple of Trump campaign rallies, and they continued as he vied for reelection. Consider a June 2020 Supreme Court ruling that essentially allowed the Trump administration to expedite deportation proceedings, paving the way for a fast-track cycle of removal (Narea). In a Pew Research Report, analysts found that arrests of undocumented people in the United States rose 30% in 2017, soon after Trump took office (Gramlich). Undoubtedly looking for an angle that would resonate with contemporary viewers, the *Party of Five* creators, it seemed, reimagined the series straight from the headlines, joining shows such as Netflix's *13 Reasons Why* (2017–20), which have unpacked the intersections of being a Latinx teen and dealing with deportation and family separation.

What is more, we need to consider timing: after just one season, Freeform announced in April 2020 that the show would not be renewed for a second season. According to the *Hollywood Reporter*, the show garnered an average of 250,000 live viewers; this does not account for the number of viewers who streamed in off hours, as we did (Goldberg). *Party of Five* also concluded its first season in early March 2020, at the beginning of the COVID-19 crisis, a pandemic of historic proportions, a time when folks were looking to the TV to pass the time at home. TV provides a much-needed distraction, and streaming networks were looking to cash in on the hours and hours of couch time. There's an issue, however. How could *Party of Five* effectively offer hours of distraction when the show's very premise, the government-enforced separation of a Mexican American family and its chaotic aftermath, was occurring in real life? This is arguably the most significant, complicated difference between the original series and its reboot. Needless to say, as fans of the show and as scholars who are deeply invested in media that treats Latinx teenagers with care and compassion, as *Party of Five* did, we were disappointed and saddened to learn of its cancellation. We can never know the full story behind its cancellation, but we do wonder what it means that the first major television series whose entire plot connected to actual, real-life consequences of inhumane immigration policies couldn't be saved, even with the original's successful history in its stead.

When the original series aired, we could count on one thing: no matter the tragedy surrounding the orphaned Salinger children, their middle-class white privilege saved the day. It's not surprising that in the original series, even as it showed the precariousness with which their lives were now lived, Charlie, Bailey, Julia, Claudia, and Owen could still engage in "normal" activities like dating, schoolwork, college, and other rites of passage. The bills somehow got paid. Emilio, Beto, Lucia, Valentina, and Rafael Acosta may still date, lose their virginity, and attend school, but these seemingly "normal" activities and daily actions are haunted by their parents' absence, with the very scary, all-too-real possibility that they will never be reunited. As the eldest, Emilio's life as sudden caretaker and manager of his parents' Mexican restaurant means his dreams of being a musician are temporarily on hold, and finances become a daily source of profound anxiety, even resentment. Emilio's status as a DACA holder also means his life is in limbo, an additional factor that clouds his responsibilities as caretaker, restaurant manager, and aspiring musician.

*Party of Five* delves into a number of important themes, including trauma; the complications of trying to maintain a sense of order in a chaotic time; and the overwhelming anxieties of living in the Trump era. While these issues impact each character in varying ways, we especially see how they manifest through the eldest daughter, fifteen-year-old Lucia.

To distract and distance herself from the pains of being separated from her family, Lucia's burgeoning queerness and immigration activism emerge side by side. One day after school, Lucia stumbles upon a deportation. As she stands to the side, in shock and unsure of what to do, an immigrant-rights activist, Sully, takes control of the situation, telling the ICE officers that they can't apprehend anyone on private property without a warrant. Sully tells Lucia to film the incident on her phone because filming is proof. Whereas Lucia wasn't present when her parents were detained, in this instance she takes on agency to help protect an undocumented man who may as well have been her father. This experience proves transformative for her. She realizes that she is passionate about immigration activism and that perhaps a career as an immigration lawyer is the most suitable career path for this young Latina who has the perfect mix of book smarts and street smarts. Lucia's passion and anger in this moment undoubtedly stem from her own feelings of powerlessness. Her passion for activism serves as a cover, in many ways, to confront the pain and intense sadness she feels for her parents' absence. Lucia is at a moment in time when she is trying to figure out who she is, and her parents' absence adds another layer of complexity. Essentially, the question she begins to ask herself is whether this activism is in vain. Does it even matter? Will it actually return her parents? Nevertheless, it is undeniable that she finds strength in immigration reform to try to understand herself and fix the problem that separated her from her parents. She continues to fight.

To learn more about helping the undocumented community, Lucia needs someone to educate her, and who better than Sully? As Lucia quickly learns, Sully is an out-and-proud queer woman who passionately leads an immigrant-rights organization. While the job might be difficult and afford few luxuries for her life, it's her calling. Sully begins to teach Lucia the ins and outs of community organizing and the legal realities facing undocumented peoples. Along the way, Lucia develops feelings for Sully, not fully understanding where admiration ends and affection begins. Although *Party of Five* hinted at Lucia's queerness early on in the season, in this instance Lucia truly comprehends that, despite her parents giving her everything and then some, they didn't give her a roadmap for knowing how to deal with her feelings for another woman, much less an adult. Her burgeoning queerness is a source of profound frustration for her, as she is unable truly to admit to herself what these feelings mean, especially when she suffers the disappointment of first love after Sully gently turns her down.

Her journey is shadowed by her budding friendship with Matthew, an undocumented trans boy. As Lucia learns about immigrant rights, she continually tries to help him, getting him a job at the Acosta family restaurant and trying to get him legal residence in the United States through the DACA program. Matthew continually tells her that DACA isn't an option for him, and, when Lucia pries, he comes out as trans. His documents only have his dead name, an identity that he will never return to. Matthew's coming out is an awakening of sorts for Lucia, who, perhaps for the first time in her life, has a meaningful conversation with a queer person about identity. She asks him how he knew. She wants to learn more about her friend, but she also wants to understand her feelings better. No one prepared her for this moment. This is yet another aspect of what made *Party of Five* special and rare for primetime TV—its attention to the complexities of being undocumented and queer, honoring the undocuqueer activists and artists like Julio Salgado who show how queerness and immigration status overlap.

During the Acosta siblings' climactic trip to Mexico to see their parents, Lucia accidentally outs herself to her mom. Her mom, always the perceptive one in the family, recognizes that Lucia is in love. When she probes her daughter, Lucia decides to tell the truth, albeit it with modified pronouns. "She" becomes "he" until Lucia gets too far deep into her story and slips up, forgetting the ruse and correctly referring to Sully as "she." To fix her problem, Lucia decides to lose her virginity with a Honduran boy who is traveling to the border with the hopes of a better life in the United States. Despite their amicable connections, Lucia's reasoning is twofold. On the one hand, she wants to get caught so that her mother will know she is "straight" and into boys. As the two start making out at the motel's pool, Lucia is preoccupied with it being a very public display with the hopes of being seen, because to be seen is to be straight. On the other hand, Lucia thinks that going through with this monumental act will "fix" her. When he suggests that they relocate to somewhere more private, she agrees. She ends up losing her virginity to him, believing that having sex with this boy will be a corrective of sorts and distract herself from her growing attraction toward Sully. When they are finished, he is glowing, and she shrinks into herself. Having sex with a boy doesn't do the trick. It just makes Lucia remorseful.

Although *Party of Five*'s abrupt cancellation left us with many unknowns about Lucia's journey through queerhood, family, and activism, the series does leave us on a positive note. Back in California, Lucia attends a protest and helps her activist friends hold down the line. She links hands with the others and smiles. She is going to be okay. She will figure out her identity and she will fiercely defend the undocumented community. Lucia will be the change she wishes to see in the world. *Party of Five*, despite its short run, was transformational television. The humanity and relatability of the Acosta family is undeniable, but, beyond that, it was the first time in recent television history where we witnessed a TV show directly confront real-life issues from the perspective of young people. Even as it explored the everyday activities of teenagers, like boring classes and homework, it refused to allow viewers to "forget" why the Acosta siblings are parentless, making us question the cruelty of family separation policies. By blurring the parameters of fiction and truth, *Party of Five* deftly explored the politics of Latinx adolescence during yet another dark chapter in our country's history.

## Adolescent Queerness and Ambivalent Latinidad: *Love, Victor*

In 2018 *Love, Simon* debuted on the big screen. The much-anticipated film adaptation of Becky Albertalli's best-selling YA novel *Simon vs. the Homo Sapiens Agenda* (2015) was immediately met with praise for its portrayal of teen Simon Spier's coming-out experience. It became one of the first big-budget Hollywood films to center a gay teen and, accordingly, was a landmark moment for LGBTQ representation in film. Yet, despite the film's accolades and success, *Love, Simon* did receive its fair share of criticism, namely that the picture perfect world of Simon Spier was filled with privilege. Simon's whiteness informs much of the story. Although he struggles with coming to terms with his identity, he enjoys many of the privileges that his whiteness affords. His family is firmly middle class and resides in an impressive home in the fictional Atlanta suburb of Creekwood. The ease of Simon's racial and class privileges extends into his coming-out experience. Although he is outed at his school, Simon faces little to no homophobia. Any potential bigotry is erased, and, in Simon's most feared act (i.e. coming out to his parents), his parents openly accept him. At every turn, Simon has it easy. And, while this certainly is not the norm for queer teens, it's Simon's experience (indeed, Simon is a white male at the end of the day, and privilege is the name of the game).

Seemingly aware of *Love, Simon*'s whiteness problems, Becky Albertalli has continued expanding the Simonverse to include teens outside of the norm. For example, in the *Simon vs. the Homo Sapiens Agenda* sequel, *Leah on the Offbeat* (2018), readers get to know Simon's friend Leah Burke, who deals with bisexuality, self-esteem, body image, and generally feeling like an outsider. Leah falls in love with Abby Suso, a Black girl who just so happens to be dating Leah's friend Nick. Other such Simonverse spinoffs include *The Upside of Unrequited* (2017) and *Love, Creekwood* (2020). Another key intervention into the Simonverse is the Hulu series *Love, Victor*, which debuted in June 2020. The show was immediately successful, becoming the most-

"I want you to know me. Who I really am"

37

watched drama series on Hulu during its initial week. In the streaming world where binging is where it's at, audiences indeed binged *Love, Victor* in its first month, making the series a critical intervention into teen representation on television (Harnick).

*Love, Victor* tells the story of Victor Salazar (played by Michael Cimino), a fifteen-year-old Puerto Rican who finds himself in Creekwood after his family's unexpected and sudden departure from Texas. Victor shares many of Simon's struggles, but there are several noticeable differences. Where Simon basked in privilege, Victor does not. Victor doesn't just struggle with coming out; he struggles to understand his sexuality. Once he realizes he is gay, he is afraid of coming out to his conservative, religious parents (particularly his uber-masculine father), who have made it very clear that homosexuality is not acceptable. The show was originally made for Disney+ but was later dropped from the new platform as it was still deciding what its brand identity was. Apparently too queer and too Latinx, *Love, Victor* moved to Hulu, where its depiction of queer teens feels a bit watered down. Oddly enough, in 2020, Disney+ debuted *Diary of a Future President*, which makes a more concerted effort to center Latinidad and deals with queerness in a way that feels incredibly fresh for Disney.

Now in Creekwood, Victor can reinvent himself a bit. On his first day at Creekwood High School he learns about the now-legendary Simon Spier, who had a whirlwind romance that even involved a much-discussed first kiss on a Ferris wheel. Victor realizes that he just might be able to be himself in this new environment, but he soon realizes that, where Simon persevered, he stumbles. Victor takes his frustration out by messaging Simon on Instagram. He writes, "Dear Simon. . . . And I just want to say—screw you! . . . For some of us it's not that easy. Screw you for having the world's most perfect, accepting parents, the world's most supportive friends. . . . I just need you to know that you're very lucky, Simon." Here is the backbone of the show. *Love, Victor* is a corrective of *Love, Simon. Love, Victor* will address issues facing queer teens of color that *Love, Simon* didn't even begin to address. And, not surprisingly, Simon really is perfect. To guide Victor on this journey is none other than Simon, who generously responds to Victor's initial message and becomes his own gay guru to help Victor work through his conflicts. Despite Victor's aggressive messages at the onset of their epistolary friendship, Simon is only interested in being the identity muse that he so desperately lacked when he was at Creekwood.

Victor finds immediate success at Creekwood, but, the more successful he becomes, the further away he is from embracing his gayness. He makes the varsity basketball team, starting at point guard. He gets along with the most popular girl in school, Mia, whom he ends up dating as he tries to understand his feelings and admiration for her. All the while, he develops a crush on Benji, an openly gay boy with whom he works at a coffee shop because he needs money to afford the $500 fee to play basketball.

Quickly becoming the popular new kid, Victor tries to balance living his truth with being the all-American boy next door, not unlike Simon. With his all-Americanness comes the social pressure and internalized homophobia to date Mia. His relationship with Mia gets increasingly uncomfortable as the show progresses. He values her friendship, and their relationship seems genuine. Even so, dating Mia is safe. He can pass as straight, and as such the relationship becomes a security blanket and a way to survive. No one will suspect the star basketball player dating Creekwood's resident "it" girl of being gay. While the show potentially could have tackled bisexuality, *Love, Victor* doesn't tread in those waters. In the end, as progressive as the show is in terms of Latinx teen representation, it really isn't meant to be *that* progressive.

Rather, *Love, Victor* pushes against the mythology of white gayness and how attractive, white gays are the default. Victor's queerness is framed as *not* being white. Moreover, the show suggests that his home environment will not allow his sexuality to exist and that his salvation and quest for answers lie with Simon. Having reached the breaking point, Victor secretly escapes to New York City to meet Simon, who is off at college living what appears to be a fantasy that Victor so desperately longs for. Upon Victor's arrival in NYC, Simon's boyfriend, Bram (of Ferris-wheel-kiss fame), meets him. Although he has some bad news (Simon is out of town), he also has some good news (he has some fun plans for Victor). Victor soon meets Simon and Bram's friend group, entirely composed of queer and trans folks. As warm and welcoming as they are, Victor doesn't know if he is in the right place. Aside from his crush, Benji, Victor doesn't really know any queer people. Is this what being gay looks like? Does he have to like drag or be able to reference the latest Lady Gaga album to fit in with queer folks? Seeing Victor's discomfort, Bram takes him to an outdoor basketball league, primarily filled with athletic men of color, including Bram, who is Black. After they hoop, Bram reveals that this is a queer basketball league. Victor, in shock, can't comprehend that these masculine athletes are gay. He learns an important lesson—there is no single way to be gay. Athletes can be gay. Masculine Black men can be gay. And Latinx men, just like Victor, can also be gay. What is more important than trying to fit into a preconceived identity is being true to yourself. Whiteness doesn't have to be the default for gay men. There is room for Victor, something he desperately needed to understand before his return to reality (aka Creekwood).

Back in Creekwood, Victor comes out to his best friend, Felix, kisses Benji (which Mia sees), and unexpectedly comes out to his parents in the first season's cliffhanger ending. Although the show might not be groundbreaking and has its share of shortcomings, it is significant in several ways. Victor's sexuality isn't slowly revealed. Rather, audiences know going in that the show is about a gay Latino boy. It's singular in that regard. Whereas other queer Latinx teens on television such as *Glee*'s Santana do not necessarily drive the show forward, Victor's gayness is the actual premise of the show.

Notably, the show is based on a concept by Albertalli and led by showrunners Isaac Aptaker and Elizabeth Berger, and none of them are Latinx. Even so, the show does raise some complicated issues about Latinidad, Latinx patriarchy, and gender. During one of our marathon texting sessions while watching some of the early episodes, Cristina complained to Trevor: "I can't with the patriarchy!" While this sentiment was undoubtedly laden with frustration and impatience, was Cristina on to something? Because, for all its wonderful attributes, we question how Victor's two models of distinctly *Latinx* masculinity—his father and grandfather—are openly homophobic, congratulate Victor on his "conquest" in winning Mia's heart, and more often than not align masculinity with heterosexual virility. In one of the first reviews of the series, Frederick Luis Aldama lamented how the series problematically "naturalizes hetero-wealth as the aspirational bar in realizing one's full potentiality as a Latinx" ("Love, Victor").

The underlying message, at least within the first season (and we are cautiously optimistic that the second season will correct these shortcomings), is that Victor must attempt to embody Simon's queer whiteness because Latinidad allows no room for queer teens like him. Essentially, Latinidad = heterosexuality and "correct" codes of masculinity. Whiteness = queerness. Of course, we know this is a facade. Victor is not white and will never be white, and this equation falsely constructs white folks as inherently accepting of queerness and Latinxs as inherently homophobic.

## Conclusion

In the pilot of Roberto Aguirre-Sacasa's reimagining of the Archie comic universe, *Riverdale* (2017–present), Veronica Lodge rolls into town, quickly making friends with Archie, Betty, and Jughead. This Veronica is still the same old Veronica from the comics—attractive, rich, fashionable, the definitive trendsetter and "it" girl of Riverdale High School. Yet this Veronica for the twenty-first century received one significant update. Played by Camila Mendes, *Riverdale*'s Veronica is a proud Latina. She speaks Spanish and forges a rum empire in Riverdale (because, well, why not?). Although Veronica's Latinidad is primarily manifested through Mendes's body and the use of Spanish phrases here and there, Veronica is Latina precisely because she can be. She doesn't have to explain or justify it. Whereas Latinx TV characters from the turn of the century such as *That '70s Show*'s Fez had to routinely defend their Latinidad, Veronica Lodge is just Veronica Lodge. She's a Latina teen living and thriving in Riverdale. As Veronica demonstrates, in addition to the teens discussed in this chapter from *On My Block*; *Party of Five*; *Love, Victor*; and *Diary of a Future President*, there has never been a better time for teenage Latinidad on the small screen. Teen Latinx characters are updating the narrative of U.S. popular culture by presenting myriad ways to be Latinx teens. In the end, there is neither one way, nor is there a rubric. Just like the real world, these TV teens kick major butt and frustrate us all at the same time, and, for us, that makes for great TV.

For further viewing:

- *The Baby-Sitters Club* (Netflix, 2020–)
- *East Los High* (Hulu, 2013–17)
- *Elena of Avalor* (Disney Channel, 2016–20)

- *Euphoria* (HBO, 2020–)
- *The Expanding Universe of Ashley Garcia* (Netflix, 2020–)
- *The Fosters* (Freeform, 2013–18)
- *Modern Family* (ABC, 2009–20)
- *Mr. Iglesias* (Netflix, 2019–)
- *Never Have I Ever* (Netflix, 2020–)
- *One Day at a Time* (Netflix/POP, 2017–20)
- *Saved by the Bell* (Peacock, 2020–)
- *13 Reasons Why* (Netflix, 2017–20).

## Scholarship on Latinx TV

Aldama, Frederick Luis and Christopher González. *Reel Latinxs: Representation in U.S. Film and TV*. The University of Arizona Press, 2019.

Aldama, Frederick Luis. *The Routledge Companion to Latina/o Popular Culture*. Routledge, 2016.

Aldama, Frederick Luis and William Anthony Nericcio. *Talking #browntv: Latinas and Latinos on the Screen*. Ohio State University Press, 2019.

Beltrán, Mary C. and Camilla Fojas, eds. *Mixed Race Hollywood*. New York University Press, 2008.

Beltrán, Mary. *Latino TV: A History*. New York University Press, 2022.

González, Tanya and Eliza Rodríguez y Gibson. *Humor and Latina/o Camp in* Ugly Betty: *Funny Looking*. Lexington Books, 2015.

Molina-Guzmán, Isabel. *Latinas & Latinos on TV: Colorblind Comedy in the Post-racial Network Era*. University of Arizona Press, 2018.

Noriega, Chon. *Shot in America: Television, the State, and the Rise of Chicano Cinema*. University of Minnesota Press, 2000.

# 2

# "DO YOU WANT TO BE A PAPI CHULO OR A PAPI FEO?"

## Latinx Teens on the Big Screen

Teen films are nothing new. In decades past, writer and director John Hughes was known for creating films that revolved around teenagers and completely revolutionized how we thought about youth. Not to mention the fact that most of his films became cult classics that regularly air on TV cable channels like TNT and TBS, so there's no escaping them. Films like *Sixteen Candles* (1984), *The Breakfast Club* (1985), and *Ferris Bueller's Day Off* (1986) all elevated teenage angst to an art, representing teens as a misunderstood lot and grownups as out of touch with the realities of youth and growing up. Core plot lines typically involved authoritarian school principals who yearned for nothing more than to squelch teen rebellion. Parents also didn't fare too well either, often portrayed as distracted, easily manipulated, and all too clueless about their children's escapades. While these films may make us laugh out loud and have inspired countless memes and expressions, there is nevertheless an obvious, glaring omission: none of these films features Latinx teenagers, often relying on racial and gender stereotypes to privilege and center white adolescence. It would take decades for Latinx teens to finally make it to the big screen in larger numbers, although, as this book has argued throughout, this group has not yet achieved racial parity when it comes to representation.

In the 1990s, however, African American filmmakers were instrumental in pushing back against racist stereotypes in Hollywood, creating films that offered complex representations of teenagers while offering critical commentary on white supremacist violence that threatens the lives and dreams of college for young Black people. Celebrated films like *Boyz n The Hood* (1991) and *Menace II Society* (1993) were in many ways a response to the Hughes 80s classics that seldom featured teens of color or often reduced them to comedic punchlines. These critical films boosted the careers of actors like Cuba Gooding Jr., Ice Cube, and Regina King, who are all household names now. Films such as these hold the power to launch careers, with some of these actors getting their breaks in roles that were cast for teens. Late 2000s films like *Dope* (2015) continue the work of these groundbreaking 90s films, this time adding humor to reflect on being a teenager of color in South Central Los Angeles.

By the early 2000s, we would likewise begin to witness a breakthrough in Latinx film representation, particularly that which chronicled adolescent storylines. From feature films to documentaries, Latinx adolescents have been the subject of powerful storylines that are long overdue. The films we engage in this chapter examine what we consider to be "typical" teenage experiences such as romantic interests, college aspirations, family, and sexuality, but, unlike those classic Hughes films that erase Latinidad and thus center whiteness, these films make front and center the teenagers' lives through a specific Latinx lens. Even as the teens all grapple with navigating common tropes like first loves, we cannot separate Latinidad from these experiences. In *Real Women Have Curves* (2002), *Raising Victor Vargas* (2002), *Mosquita y Mari* (2012), and *Spider Man: Into the Spider-Verse* (2018), the teen characters offer profound expressions of Latinx adolescence as they maneuver uncharted waters around love, college, saving the world, trauma, and race. Further, we want to reference the incredible documentary work that has been done to legitimize Latinx adolescents as rightful protagonists. Important work, including *Precious Knowledge* (2011) and *Colossus* (2018), for example, center the stories of young Latinxs through first-person interviews and dialogue, powerful contributions to filmic representations of youth of color that warrant further scholarly attention.

## Literature Review: On "Bad Hombres" and "Sexy Spitfires"

To discuss Latinx film and the presence of Latinxs in film, we have to begin with Hollywood's infamous history of stereotyping. While our students may grow tired of this conversation ("It's just a movie, Professor!"), we must document this history because of its insidious nature. It's not "just" a movie, and the stereotypes visible in these films are not simply harmless or "all in good fun." Instead, as film scholar Charles Ramírez Berg explains:

> The case of Latino stereotyping in mass media involves a discursive system that might be called 'Latinism' (a play on Edward Said's Orientalism): the construction of Latin America and its inhabitants and of Latinos in this country to justify the United States' imperialistic goals. Operationalized externally as the Monroe Doctrine and internally as Manifest Destiny, U.S. imperialism was based on the notion that the nation should control the entire hemisphere and was willing to fight anyone who disagreed.... On the whole, Hollywood endorsed North American dominance of this hemisphere, and as often as it depicted that hegemony uncritically, movies helped to perpetuate it. (4)

Hollywood actually benefited from colonialism, and it's not surprising that early twentieth-century films often featured "savage" Latinx characters who threatened the "goodness" of America, which was in need of rescue by an Anglo hero. For many decades, the only way that non-Latinxs knew or heard about Latinxs was through film, where men were bandidos and women were seductive temptresses. If you only see the stereotype, then it is what you will believe. This is especially pertinent when we consider the intersections between media stereotyping and youth-of-color identities, although, to be sure, adults are impacted by these images as well (Shafer and Rivadeneyra 2). Mid-twentieth-century films starring John Wayne invoked this nostalgia for the supposed "good ole days" of American imperialism.

In addition to outright promoting the United States as a "superior" country whose fate is tied to global and hemispheric domination and power, early films ushered in a number of stereotypes and flawed portrayals of Latinxs that we continue to see today. According to Ramírez Berg, "The history of Latino images in U.S. cinema is in large measure a pageant of six basic stereotypes: el bandido, the harlot, the male buffoon, the female clown, the Latin lover, and the dark lady" (66). While we may consider these to be "old" stereotypes that have little, if anything, to do with our contemporary reality, these tropes continue to manifest in the present day. The late, great Lupe Ontiveros revealed in multiple interviews before her death that she was cast as a maid in both film and television at least one hundred fifty times throughout her career (*NPR*). Without a doubt, Ontiveros carried herself with dignity given the limited opportunities that came her way, but, like her, we lament that this role was the primary one that was offered to her. We do not begrudge actors for taking these roles, but we do take aim at Hollywood's history of white supremacy, which has seldom considered talented Latinx actors for more complicated roles. As we teach our students, when we constantly see films in which Latinx actors are cast through such a narrow lens, we come to believe that these are the only acceptable roles in which *all* living and breathing Latinx people should be seen. For example, in their study on television stereotypes and their effects on Latinx "emerging adults," Jessie Shafer and Rocío Rivadeneyra found that exposure to these media images can potentially impact youth self-esteem (5). While the authors of this study point out that "stereotypes do not impact all people in the same way" (5), their research confirms that stereotypes are not a "simple" matter but are far more complex in youth Latinx interactions with them. It comes as no surprise, then, that many of our students, Latinx and non-Latinx, have registered shock that there is such a thing as complex Latinx representation on the page, stage, and big and small screens.

While authentic representation is part of the problem, perhaps more so is representation overall, considering that in the "2018 UCLA Hollywood Diversity Report, of the top two hundred films produced in 2016, Latinx actors were featured in only 2.7 percent of the film roles" (Fregoso 484). This grim number is even more stark when we consider that the Latinx community "make[s] up one of the most reliable and largest blocks of moviegoers" (Aldama and González 11). The issue is thus twofold: Latinxs are rarely featured in major roles, and when they are they often are still portrayed in ways that uncover Hollywood's ugly history of stereotyping Latinxs as tricksters, seductresses, or ridiculous clowns. Although we've stated this a number of times throughout this book, it bears repeating that these stereotypes have actual ramifications in real life. Case in point: Donald Trump's 2016 White House bid, a campaign that built its entire platform on tapping into white fears over all those "bad hombres" and "taco trucks on every corner" that could only signal the downfall of the United States as we know it. Our love of tacos aside, Trump's rhetoric in many ways harkened back to the early days of Hollywood cinema, proving once again that stereotypes are never simply a matter of entertainment.

In response to this double-edged sword, Latinx filmmakers, writers, and artists have worked extra hard to counter this troubling history through complex representations and scripts that resist simplistic renderings of Latinidad, seen in the films we discuss in this chapter. Sure, these teens may get into trouble. They talk back to their parents. They lose their virginity against their parents' wishes. They might sneak out of the house from time to time. But the films allow them to make mistakes in honest, relatable ways that do not necessitate falling into the stereotype trap for the storylines to unravel. Even in films by non-Latinx writers and directors, like *Girlfight* (2000) and *Mi Vida Loca* (1993), the adolescent characters have room to grow, make mistakes, and come into their own. As scholars and movie buffs, we yearn for this kind of representation, and this is precisely why we're big fans of the movies we discuss in this chapter. The teens are messy at times, funny and rebellious, and one is even a superhero, showing us that Latinx adolescents, when portrayed in complex, well-rounded ways, make for great entertainment at the box office.

As this book demonstrates, we need complex, multidimensional representation of Latinx teenagers that real-life young people can interact and engage with, and this is not solely to validate and affirm Latinx adolescents, although this of course is hugely important, but, beyond that, critical representation offers Latinxs of all ages an opportunity truly to grasp what it means to be a young person of color in the twenty-first century, a century that has witnessed rampant school shootings; 9/11; incredible technological innovations, for better or worse; inspiring protest movements like Black Lives Matter; and the presidential election of a failed businessman turned reality-TV personality. Take, for example, writer and director Cruz Ángeles's 2009 film *Don't Let Me Drown*, which takes place in the few short months post 9/11 in Brooklyn, New York. In this beautiful and touching film, we witness the tender love grow between teenage Mexican American Lalo (E.J. Bonilla) and Dominican American Stefanie (Gleendilys Inoa), whose sister was killed in the Twin Towers attack. One of the few films that takes on the 9/11 attacks from a specific Latinx adolescent point of view, Ángeles's film takes great care to treat the teenagers with compassion as they grapple with trauma, anti-Blackness, domestic violence, and poverty. Although not written or directed by Latinxs, Richard Glatzer and Wash Westmoreland's 2006 film *Quinceañera* deftly traces Magdalena's (Emily Ríos) struggle with a secret pregnancy on the verge of her fifteenth birthday, a period of life that corresponds with her queer cholo cousin Carlos's (Jesse García) banishment from the family. Magdalena and Carlos come together in their shared exile from their families, demonstrating the power of "creating familia from scratch," as Cherríe Moraga calls it. Both films, like the ones we discuss in this chapter, complicate Latinx adolescence by treating the hopes, dreams, fears, and realities of young people with the seriousness they deserve. Even as the films deal with complex tropes like domestic violence and teen pregnancy, the films are not clichéd. Instead, we as viewers see these critical issues directly impact Latinx teenagers whose coming-of-age is messy, traumatizing, and intermittently filled with the joys of first love and shared bonds of loyalty.

## Chicana Adolescence, Sexuality, and Bodily Love: *Real Women Have Curves*

Today, audiences recognize America Ferrera as one of film and TV's most well-known Latina actors. Her breakout performances in *The Sisterhood of the Traveling Pants* (2005), *Ugly Betty* (2006–10), and *Superstore* (2015–21) have helped normalize Latina experiences that push against stereotypes and, accordingly, give young girls new identity scripts to follow. But, before she became a household name, Ferrera got her start in a definitively Chicana vehicle—*Real Women Have*

*Curves*, Patricia Cardoso's 2002 film based on Josefina López's largely autobiographical play of the same name.

*Real Women* follows high schooler Ana Garcia (Ferrera) and a group of Mexicanas working under oppressive conditions in her sister Estela's East Los Angeles sewing factory. While Ana dreams of becoming a writer, her sister worries about keeping her business afloat amid the swirling threats of being deported by La Migra. All the while, Ana grows as a budding Chicana feminist. She wants to go to college in New York City and distance herself from her mother Carmen's (Lupe Ontiveros) patriarchal hand. Although Ana's aspirations are central to the film's plot, the film also gives us glimpses into Estela's role as the eldest child who must stay behind and help support her family. Estela's disappointments are only hinted at, but in these small moments the film also sheds light on the dutiful role that Estela is expected to carry on, which Ana vocally protests. Ana attends high school across town in Beverly Hills where she is mentored by her teacher, played by George Lopez, who sees her full potential. At school she meets Jimmy, who recognizes her inner and outer beauty, two things that have been the subject of harsh criticism by Ana's mother. In the end, Ana leaves Los Angeles and begins a new life as a college student in New York City. While the film has become canonical for a number of reasons, perhaps most significant is that the film broke ground for its portrayal of a full-figured Chicana teenager, centering bodies that have typically been rendered invisible by Hollywood.

As *Real Women* is based on Josefina López's own experiences of growing up undocumented and working in a sewing factory in Los Angeles, it allows the film to humanize undocumented people, which is often unseen in mainstream theatre. According to López, "It also reveals a dignity and humanity that is often missing in portrayals of immigrants who are always portrayed as victims rather than the heroes and heroines of their story" (qtd. in Boffone, "Immigration"). At the center of this, of course, is Ana, who is a stand-in for López as a teenager.

As Ana develops a distinctly Chicana feminist consciousness, she learns to embrace her body and reject her mother's strict demands that she go on a diet and be subservient to the men in her life. Ana loses her virginity to her white boyfriend, Jimmy, which sets up one of the more powerful and telling scenes in the film. Ana's sexual encounter with Jimmy is significant because it is she who is in complete control. She buys the condoms, arranges the engagement, and dictates how the night unfolds. She even turns the lights on so that her lover can see her as she truly is, which, as Jimmy tells her, is "que bonita." In the aftermath of their sexual encounter, Jimmy tells Ana he will write to her when he goes to college, but Ana is not interested in a pen pal. Her relationship with Jimmy is physical and is based on Ana's need for sexual discovery and awakening. The next morning, Ana opens her robe in front of the bathroom mirror to view herself as Jimmy had the previous night. This is a powerful moment that suggests that Ana is truly seeing herself for the first time and has successfully made the transition from girl to woman, from youth to adult, from undocumented to documented, from Mexican American to Chicana, and from object to subject. While she is exploring her body, Carmen enters and immediately knows that her daughter is no longer a virgin. She calls Ana a "tramp" and proclaims, "I can tell. You're not only fat, now you're a puta!" In Carmen's view, Ana does not value herself, to which Ana responds with her distinctly feminist message: "there is more to me than what's in between my legs." This emphasizes how losing one's virginity is, in fact, a political act. By rejecting cultural norms, she confirms that the personal is political and, in the process, declares that she will not be her mother's "baby anymore."

Ana's journey culminates in the film's iconic undressing scene in which Ana leads the women in the sewing factory in a ceremonial disrobing that leaves them in their underwear comparing their bodies and fat and how these physical markers affect them emotionally. When Carmen questions her daughter's actions, Ana responds, "We're all women. We all have the same," thus uniting these women via their shared experiences. In this powerful scene, Ana rejects the patriarchal mandates of modesty and vergüenza, declaring that she is not ashamed of her body. Rather than allow herself to be dictated by shame and "el qué dirán" ("what will everyone say?"), Ana flaunts her body proudly to insist on her right to bodily autonomy and agency.

López began crafting the disrobing scene while at legendary playwright and mentor María Irene Fornés's Hispanic Playwrights-in-Residence Lab at International Arts Relations (INTAR) in New York in the late 80s. Fornés taught López that "nothing is silly" and to "always go back to the image." In a 1992 interview with Jorge Huerta, López comments on how she had to work through misgivings she had about seemingly simple, "silly" things that can actually be powerful. López admits, "The characters want to take off their clothes, then let them take off their clothes, it's so Goddam hot. And so I let the characters take off their clothes" ("Huerta Interview"). The disrobing scene has become a landmark moment in American theatre and film in and of itself, as it was the first time that Latinas got to take off their clothes not to exploit their sexuality for a man's pleasure but to own their humanity.

In terms of metaphors, the undressing scene allows the women, and subsequently the film's actor, the opportunity to literally and symbolically remove all of the layers that society has imposed on them. According to theatre scholar Tiffany Ana López, even though these women's bodies have been a source of cultural wounding, they can also become sites of healing: "Ana re-presents her body to her mother so that her mother might revise her thinking by seeing the female body in a different light occupied by collective female display and viewership" ("Suturing" 301). Witnessing a full-bodied woman remove her clothes on the big screen in a positive way is a rare occurrence, and so, naturally, this scene becomes the film's signature moment and an anthem that celebrates the large Latina body. Josefina López and Patricia Cardoso emphatically declare that, yes, these bodies do exist, and they should be seen and celebrated. Naturally, this was freeing for López. Not only are the fictional women gaining autonomy over their marginalized bodies, but López, as a playwright and screenwriter, became freer and achieved a level of artistic authority that she had never tapped into. In this way, both the theatrical and metaphorical disrobing scenes become what M. Teresa Marrero has called a "symbolic act of liberation" in which these women look to each other for validation while they remove their clothes and expose their true selves to each other (69).

In many ways, *Real Women Have Curves* ushered in a new era of Latinx cinema. The film became a runaway success, winning the prestigious Audience Award for best dramatic film and the Special Jury Prize for acting in the 2002 Sundance Film Festival. *Real Women* launched America Ferrera's career and helped build López's theatre company, CASA 0101 Theater, in Boyle Heights. Notably, López was able to capitalize on the film's success and bring new audiences to CASA 0101, which is still going strong today and serves as a fundamental cultural institution in the Los Angeles enclave.

After debuting nearly two decades ago, the *Real Women* film is now seen as archetypal. For example, the critical darling of 2018, *Lady Bird*, curiously shared many similarities with *Real Women*. Intentional or not, nearly every plot point in *Lady Bird* matches that of *Real Women*. These similarities were not lost on Cardoso and López. As Rosa Linda Fregoso notes,

> A few days before the 2018 Academy Awards, Patricia Cardoso circulated a *New York Times* article comparing that year's Oscar-nominated *Lady Bird* with her *Real Women Have Curves*, which anticipated many of the mother-daughter conflicts of the former without meriting the Academy's accolades. Although *Real Women Have Curves* received rave reviews from the indie community in 2002, including being the first Latina-directed feature to be awarded Best Picture at Sundance, it was virtually ignored by the Academy's mostly white Tinseltown coterie. (Fregoso 484)

Perhaps *Real Women Have Curves* was ahead of its time. Or maybe the film's lack of recognition by mainstream Hollywood over time is more a commentary on how Latinx stories are often relegated to the sidelines. Regardless, one thing is certain—*Real Women Have Curves* paved the way for a groundswell of Latinx cinema in the twenty-first century.

## Adolescent Masculinity and Papis Chulos: *Raising Victor Vargas*

When newbie director Peter Sollett's extremely low-budget film, *Raising Victor Vargas*, was released in 2002, movie reviews described it in very similar ways: an authentic comedy that understands the awkwardness of teen dating life. Writing for the *New Yorker*, David Denby called attention to the "amateur cast" of teenagers who "speak in the profane idiom of the New York streets" ("Big Loser"), while René Rodríguez's review in *Hispanic* references its "humble, humanist center" (70). These comments take on more meaning when we understand a bit more about the film's backstory.

In his review, Rodríguez describes Sollett's process of developing a film that was cast entirely of first-time, inexperienced teen actors:

> When writer-director Peter Sollett set out to make his first film, he intended to make an autobiographical drama about growing up in his white, predominantly Italian and Jewish Brooklyn neighborhood of Bensonhurst. But after discovering he was unable to find any actors who fit that ethnic mold and were also talented enough to carry the film, Sollett broadened his net. He and producer Eva Vives put up fliers in their East Village neighborhood in New York, inviting anyone who read them to attend an open casting call. It was then that Sollett finally found his actors. The problem? They were all of Latino descent. But Sollett's story, about a street-smart kid's gradual transformation from self-obsessed teenager to a more thoughtful, aware young man, was universal enough to lend itself to any ethnicity. (70)

We reference this quotation in its entirety to reflect on what it means for a white filmmaker to create a film that was originally intended to center white adolescence but "ended up" being about a group of mainly Afro-Dominican American teenagers growing up on the Lower East Side of Manhattan. Our point is not to question whether white filmmakers like Sollett can sensitively and critically create works about Latinx teens, or whether they should at all. Indeed, films by non-Latinx creators have been hugely successful, like *Girlfight* and *Mi Vida Loca*. Instead, we ask what it means that a treasure of a film like *Raising Victor Vargas* was the end result of an entirely coincidental casting call that was answered by Latinx teenagers, essentially without any critical intentionality around creating a complex film about this overlooked and underappreciated demographic. The film is incredibly important when we consider that there is a shortage of films that feature storylines based around Latinx teenagers, but Sollett's initial take, to otherwise exclude telling a story about Latinx youth in the most diverse city in the United States, is complicated and odd to say the least. Nevertheless, we have chosen this film because of its deft portrayal of Latinx youths' masculinity, family, and feelings of rejection and belonging. Sollett's film is particularly resonant, even if the original intent evaded attempts at telling a story about Latinx youth.

The film is incredibly low budget and largely takes place around a few blocks in a Lower East Side neighborhood and in the cramped apartment where teenage Victor (Victor Rasuk) lives with his highly religious and cranky grandmother, Altagracia, and his younger siblings, Nino and Vicki. As Naida García-Crespo points out, the plot is rather straightforward in how it "present[s] the complexities of everyday life, from ostensibly innocuous gossip (e.g., Victor's relationship to Donna) to the clash of generational attitudes about sex (e.g., Altagracia's judgment of Judy and Victor)" (168). In fact, the apartment surroundings take up a large part of the film, the incredibly tight quarters symbolizing Victor's feelings of confinement in a space in which all of his actions are surveilled by his hypervigilant grandmother, who criticizes virtually everything he does while doting on the younger Nino, whom she believes she must protect from Victor's supposedly wayward tendencies.

The film begins just as the sex-starved Victor is about to sleep with a neighbor girl, crudely known in his barrio as "Fat Donna," only to be outed by his metiche friend Harold, who chides his boy for what he interprets as lowering his standards. In what appears to begin as a raunchy teenage boy film in the tradition of *Animal House* (1978) or *American Pie* (1999), *Raising Victor Vargas* surprises viewers by being far from that tired old tradition of cinematic storylines around horny teenage boys whose sole mission is to lose their virginity. Victor does indeed try to save his rep by channeling his energy into capturing the attention of the beautiful Judy, his new love interest whom he initially attempts to charm as a way of deflecting attention from his ill-fated sexual escapade with Donna.

But Judy will have none of his antics, and she rejects him at the community pool, *the* place to meet and hook up. She quite efficiently turns him down in a no-nonsense way. And again. And once more. These contrite rejections are humorous, as viewers empathize with Victor's bruised ego, his pride deflated time and time again by a smart and assertive young woman who sees right through his ridiculous pickup lines. The film, however, showcases Victor's transformation; as Rodolfo Popelnik states: "Victor actually comes to see Judy as a person and not a mere conquest spurned by his hormones" (73). The film does present what we consider to be the traditional aspects of straight, cisgender male adolescence, such as Victor's humorous but uncomplicated question to his hermanito, Nino, who asks for advice on winning over the ladies: "Do you want to be a papi chulo or a papi feo?" But what matters most in this film is Victor's development from a wannabe papi chulo into a sensitive, multidimensional young man.

Take, for example, a highly charged moment in the film, when the stubbornly rigid abuela, Altagracia, discovers that her pride and joy, Nino, has been spending a large amount of time masturbating in the bathroom, an act she blames on Victor, whom she chides for being a "bad influence" on the innocent and naïve younger brother. Frustrated, she admonishes Victor and goes straight to the Social Services office, where she tells the caseworker that she "no longer wants him in [her] house." This moment of cruelty, of utter desperation, greatly impacts Victor, who is left hurt, rejected, and confused by Altagracia's sudden attempt to evict him from their home. In many ways, this serves as a turning point for Victor, whose incredible shame and hurt leads him to show his true self to Judy. He is not simply a papi chulo, a Don Juan in the making who leads young women astray. Victor is a complex, tender, and sensitive Latino teenager who learns how to express vulnerability and love not through swagger and hypermasculinity but through gentleness and emotion.

Altagracia does relent somewhat, making him promise to attend Mass with her as a way to atone for his supposed "sins." While Altagracia's action can be described as cruel, the film takes care not to demonize her, instead highlighting how the three children in her charge are not the menaces that she initially proclaims Victor to be. Victor is not a "bad" kid who causes harm or reckless disregard, even as his early attempts to woo the reluctant Judy fall flat. Victor learns from these epic turndowns, even refusing to talk back in hateful or vengeful ways when his own grandmother threatens to evict him. In focusing on Victor's feelings of rejection and hurt from his grandmother, the film explores in powerful ways what lurks beneath the surface of an outwardly confident Latino teenager. In these subtleties and nuances, what matters most in this film is not plot but character development. It focuses less on what happens than on exploring who the characters are, with all their flaws, messy imperfections, and moments of joy. The film compassionately conveys the challenges of urban, youthful

Latinx masculinity that confronts heteropatriarchal expectations of bravado and swagger. Victor captures Judy's affections by being real, vulnerable, and honest, and in turn she tears down some of her own walls, trusting this sensitive young boy with her heart.

*Raising Victor Vargas*, unlike films like *Spider-Man: Into the Spider-Verse* or even *Real Women Have Curves*, did not achieve large box-office success, and, while we cannot begin to know why it did not make it to nationwide movie theaters, it is disheartening to know that a wonderful film is often reduced to the margins of mainstream consciousness. We all know that teenage films are a niche market and can bring loads of revenue, as is evident in the Hughes classics of the 80s to even more contemporary adolescent-themed films like *The Hunger Games* (2012) or *Twilight* (2008). But what does it mean that a touching film like *Victor Vargas*, set in similar urban landscapes of box office successes, is relatively ignored? Is it because, as Popelnik correctly asserts, "*Raising Victor Vargas* is delightfully atypical in that it does not rely on the worn thematic conventions of gangs, drugs, crime, prostitution, and poverty that normally accompany the representations made of Latinos throughout film history" (73)? Even as we witness the modesty of Victor's material surroundings, the film refuses to comment extensively on these issues, and this is incredibly refreshing, given that Latinxs historically have seldom been portrayed outside the narrative of poverty, gang violence, and crime. Instead, the film, while set within the urban landscape of the Lower East Side, traces a relatively simple story of a Dominican American teenage boy who falls in love for the first time, who struggles to please his grandmother, and who likes to kick it at the pool with his friends. In refusing to play into these old stereotypes of all Latinx teenagers as would-be gang members destined for a life of crime, the film insists on revealing universal themes like first love, family strife, and the pressures of heteronormative masculinity through the lens of Latinidad. Raising Victor Vargas may come with a set of challenges for Altagracia, but in the end we know he'll turn out alright.

## Queer Chicana Adolescence and Agency: *Mosquita y Mari*

Writing about *Mosquita y Mari* (2012) for his review in the *Hollywood Reporter*, Duane Byrge had this to say of the two teen Chicana actors who were cast for the titular roles: "As Yolanda, Fenessa Pineda delicately reveals her character's inner conflicts. As Mari, Venecia Troncoso smolders as the bad-girl-with-a-big-heart. Troncoso's sultry looks and nuanced, exuberant portrayal should attract the attention of L.A. casting agents." While his review of queer Chicana filmmaker Aurora Guerrero's work is otherwise positive, we begin with this statement because of its unsettling nature, which we have unpacked in this chapter and throughout this book. What does it mean that Byrge reduces Venecia Troncoso's performance as Mari to a character who is a "bad-girl-with-a-big-heart" who possesses "sultry looks"? Unfortunately, this simplistic assessment reveals how even young Latina actors who portray teenagers on the screen are not spared from the incredibly sexist and racist history of film in this country. Guerrero's deeply touching, important film that centers young, queer Chicana voices is exactly the kind of work that claps back to this problematic history, as it demands a more critical and sympathetic view of Chicana teens as they determine their own bodily, sexual agency as queer Chicana subjects.

An independent film released in 2012 at the celebrated Sundance Film Festival, *Mosquita y Mari* tells the story of two fifteen-year-old Chicanas who meet in their high school geometry class in Huntington Park, California. A predominantly Latinx, working-class, immigrant community (indeed, Cristina has family who live in Huntington Park), Huntington Park is beautifully imagined in Guerrero's film as the site of young, burgeoning queer first love between two young Chicanas. Although films like Peter Bratt's *La Mission* reflect an inability to imagine Latinx queers as inhabiting and navigating multiple urban spaces—signaling what cultural studies scholar Richard T. Rodriguez suggests is an implied "strict geographical divide between Latinx space and queer space" (456)—*Mosquita y Mari* refutes this separation in its representation of the queer girls' mobility within and outside of their community. This urban backdrop is crucial, as at times the film simply captures quiet moments in the community and at other times its busy sites of commerce. In these deliberate, intentional shots of the community, Guerrero queers Latinx urban spaces to insist on the presence of young Chicanas who maneuver them to survive *and* thrive.

At the center of the film are the two girls who couldn't possibly be any more different. Yolanda is affectionately nicknamed Mosquita (which means a "little fly") for persistently "buzzing around" in her efforts to tutor the skeptical, resistant Mari in geometry. An unlikely friendship ensues between the straight-A student Yolanda, whose proud but conservative parents prominently display her 100% test scores on the refrigerator, and Mari, the daughter of a widowed mother who struggles to make ends meet after their father dies. The film subtly but powerfully unveils the growing attraction between Yolanda and Mari as their friendship ventures into uncharted territory. Yolanda is the friendly, eager teacher's pet, and Mari is the quiet, guarded new kid who can't understand why Yolanda enjoys such a boring subject like math, but, ever so slowly and humorously, Mari lets down her guard, giving Yolanda glimpses into her home life, one that is riddled by the anxiety of watching her mother struggle to make rent and her subsequent guilt over this fact.

Their bond begins to take shape through the sort of typical teen girl rite of passage that cements their friendship; they take a photo together in a local studio, no smiles of course, no doubt an homage to the photoshoots that were incredibly popular among teens of color in the 90s. The photo leads to other queer, subtly erotic moments. They share an ice-cream cone. They nap on the couch, legs and bodies intertwined, and share an almost-kiss until Yolanda's helicopter parents show up and kill the moment. They dance a cumbia, and Yolanda dons a cowboy hat to signal that this is not just a dance between two friends. It's a courtship, but it's one that's never spoken aloud but rather hinted at, shyly at first, the girls oh so close to revealing their feelings to each other but never actually arriving at the moment, since what matters most for the film is the subtleties, the feelings, the tensions, and the chemistry between the girls.

In his astute analysis of the film, Arturo Aldama discusses how the teen girls navigate their homes and communities that reinforce "compulsory heteronormative practices that are usually the subject of the double-standard gaze for many Latinx families" (124). Not surprisingly, then, when Yolanda scores the rare lower-than-an-A grade on a geometry test, her hypervigilant parents presume that it must be the result of her distraction with a wayward, anonymous muchacho without shame. We viewers, of course, know that this nameless sin vergüenza does not exist, but her parents' insistence on uncovering the supposed "truth" of their daughter's heterosexual teen hormones shows the tricky waters that queer teen girls must navigate, between the pressures of "el qué dirán" that Aldama addresses and trying to honor the feelings bubbling up inside. In a powerful moment, Guerrero deftly conveys these external pressures in a scene where the two girls sit in an abandoned car and Mari rebelliously and playfully writes in dust, "Mosquita y Mari and fuck the rest." This moment is undeniably queer, the simple "y" uniting them against the world while offering a simple but powerful rejection of community, peer, and familial pressures to perform heterosexual and obedient girlhood.

A common question Cristina's students ask when she screens the film is how this work can be queer if the girls don't ever utter the words *queer* or *lesbian* or *gay*. But this is the beauty of Guerrero's filmmaking. The girls don't have to profess their growing love and attraction to each other to know the feelings are there. The film's power rests more on the subtleties, what is not said over what is said, to document how it is the friendship between the two young women and "the intimacy of these relationships that often provides the context for lesbian desire" (Esquibel 91). For film studies scholar Whitney Monaghan, the question asked by Cristina's students demonstrates how, far too often, queer girls on screen are represented through "the common trope of *coming out as coming of age* [that] sees queer youth coming of age only by coming to terms with their sexuality and/or gender identity and verbally articulating it" (99, original italics). Yolanda and Mari don't need to vocally express their queerness to be queer; instead, "In stark contrast to the confessional, dialogue-focused *coming out as coming of age* narrative, the unspoken is taken up in *Mosquita y Mari* on both a narrative and stylistic level" (Monaghan 104, original italics). What matters most is their growing bond, a union that they know their families and school friends will delegitimize.

In a climactic scene in the film, however, Guerrero critically documents the many survival strategies employed by teen girls of color in communities throughout the world. In the case of Mari, it's exchanging sex with an older Chicano boy who relentlessly follows her around the neighborhood because he has marked her as a potential conquest. Unlike her affectionate nickname for the pleasantly annoying Mosquita, whose presence is sincere and rooted in admiration, this older boy's lingering body is instead tinged with violence, danger, and exploitation. And exploit is exactly what he does to Mari, manipulating her vulnerability and desperation for rent money, which he provides on the condition that she have sex with him. Mosquita witnesses the minutes after this exchange, which ultimately leads to many questions about the future of their relationship. What happens next? What does the future hold for their relationship and for their queer lives? But while we may focus on this one moment of desperation, the film refuses to define Mari by this act, and it does not erase the sexual and emotional intimacy that has developed between the two girls. We don't know what exactly the future holds for Yolanda and Mari, but what does matter is the loving, tender feelings of first love that the film captures in a compassionate and validating manner.

In our chapter on Latinx teens on the small screen, we discussed the ambivalent queer Latinidad of the series *Love, Victor*, which suggests that queerness and Latinidad are incompatible. *Mosquita y Mari* centers two queer Chicanas who could be Victor's peers. They share quite a bit in common. They're young, they're queer, and they have families who expect comportment to heteronormativity. But the storylines and messaging are far from similar. While the community of Huntington Park is potentially dangerous for young girls of color, especially queer girls, writer and director Aurora Guerrero places Chicanismo front and center with queerness. The film pays homage to the visual aesthetics of cholita photo shoots; paleteros are on every corner; Spanish is freely spoken; and even Yolanda's nickname cannot be overlooked. In these crucial differences, Guerrero centralizes Chicanx queer community members while also critiquing the violent underpinnings of heteropatriarchy, sexism, and machismo that put the lives of young, queer Chicana teenagers in danger. But, despite these dangers, the girls lean on each other, revealing the beauty of their loving declaration that was first etched in dust: "Mosquita y Mari." Though written in dust, which can fly off into the wind, this statement is marked by the very particles that circulate and filter through the air, like the powerful but unspoken language of their queer first love. Their love will not be erased.

### The Afro-Latino Adolescent Hero: *Spider-Man: Into the Spider-Verse*

When *Spider-Man: Into the Spider-Verse* swung into movie theaters in 2018, it had all of the makings of the Spider-Man franchise. A New

York City teen gets bitten by a mutated spider and transforms into the iconic superhero. He learns to harness his newfound powers set against his teenage awkwardness to defeat the villain and save New York City. Yet, just like so many popular culture examples in this book, *Into the Spider-Verse* traded in the old for something new. While Peter Parker is an integral part of the film, it isn't really about him at all. It's about Miles Morales, the first Afro-Latinx Spider-Man. The film turned the genre on its head to speak to Black and Brown kids who are regularly excluded from the comic-book genre. By injecting new life into an old story, *Into the Spider-Verse* positioned Morales as a twenty-first-century superhero who actually reflected our demographics, making him incredibly relatable to young people. Film critic Carlos Aguilar acknowledges, "The sole existence of Miles Morales in the Marvel universe was a win in the fight for representation, but to have him star in one of the best-reviewed, bound-to-be-a-hit movies of the year—that's true change" (Remezcla). The film was an audience and critical success, winning the 2019 Academy Award for Best Animated Film.

Superhero films and comic-book adaptations for the big screen have seemingly always been popular, but in the twenty-first century they have been some of Hollywood's highest-grossing films. Audiences religiously flock to franchises such as the Avengers, Batman, Black Panther, Ironman, Wonder Woman, X-Men, and, of course, Spider-Man. Although these films may not win handfuls of Academy Awards, there is little doubt that they have a tremendous impact on contemporary U.S. popular culture. Superheroes are avatars that we tap into to access larger cultural ideas. Morales, in this case, enables Afro-Latinx children and teens to relate to someone like them. In an NPR interview, the film's co-director Peter Ramsey affirms, "It means a lot for young black and Latino kids to see themselves up on screen in these iconic, heroic, mythic stories. . . . It's a need being fulfilled" (Bowman and Garcia-Navarro). Miles Morales, in fact, is part of a large "Latino superhero archive," as Frederick Luis Aldama's study of Latinx comics shows us, tracing back to a Latino character in the 1940s Marvel Universe (*Latinx Superheroes* 4). Of course, we should also note that Morales is part of a rich tradition of more-updated and highly complex Latinx superheroes like America Chavez—the brainchild of Boricua writer Gabby Rivera, who created the badass queer comic in 2017—a reinvention of Marvel's Miss America, a white superhero (García 172). As so many superhero and comic-book fans do, we project ourselves onto superheroes. We see our best selves in them. And, just like us, they struggle. They face difficulties and they have insecurities. Despite his larger-than-life abilities and their corresponding responsibilities, Morales is not unlike his Spider-Man brethren. He's super nerdy. He is a misfit. He makes mistakes. He's not always embraced by the public even as he tries to save it.

Miles Morales debuted as a comic-book series in 2011 after the unexpected death of Peter Parker. The son of a Puerto Rican mother and an African American father, Morales was the first Black Spider-Man and the second Latinx Spider-Man (the first being Miguel O'Hara, aka Spider-Man 2099). *Into the Spider-Verse* doesn't begin with Morales. Rather than hearing Morales's origin story, we instead quickly learn about Peter Parker's origin story and his enormous list of contributions to popular culture. He's got a great theme song, a popsicle, and a Christmas album. Oh, and, of course, we are reminded that "with great power comes great responsibility." One doesn't simply gain superpowers without having the responsibility to use them for good. The film then cuts to Miles Morales, a smart teen who is an aspiring graffiti artist and is obsessed with comics, Spider-Man included. Rather than attend his zoned public school, Brooklyn Middle, he instead attends the academically rigorous Brooklyn Visions Academic, an "elitist" school where he doesn't necessarily fit in. While still in Brooklyn, it's a world away.

The film shifts the franchise's typical Queens setting to a Brooklyn-based storyline that foregrounds Morales's Black and Latinx roots. Despite his larger-than-life responsibilities (Hello, he *only* has to save all of humanity!), Morales still gets to be a teenager. He tags far away from his police officer father's strict surveillance. He crushes on Gwen Stacy, aka Spider Gwen. He jams to Biggie Smalls's "Hypnotize" on his headphones as he walks to school. And it is worth noting that Morales isn't simply a stand-in for diversity so that the Spider-Man franchise can meet a quota. Rather, his portrayal conveys many aspects of the Nuyorican experience. His mother, Rio Morales, speaks to him in Spanish, nagging him as mothers of teenage boys often do (according to their sons, at least). Miles responds to her in Spanish, speaking in a noticeably different way. His second-generation accent is distinct from his mother's native Puerto Rican accent, representing the evolution of the Morales family's Spanish in the United States. As Miles heads to school, he interacts with other teens in equal parts English and Spanish, code-switching effortlessly between the two. And, perhaps most significantly, none of this is subtitled. We also must recognize that Miles takes his mother's name—Morales—as opposed to his father's name (Davis), even though his parents are married. With these powerful elements, the film normalizes the Afro-Latinx adolescent experience in a subtle way; that is, by not drawing excessive attention to things like Miles's code-switching or his last name, these aspects become refreshingly *normal*, simply a part of who he is.

Moreover, he is praised for being a star student. Whether it's by his parents or his community, his intellectual curiosity is celebrated. As the editors of *Remezcla* raved soon after the film's release, "Furthermore, Miles is a person of color who doesn't come from a broken home: His parents are educated professionals and he's proud of who he is and where he comes from. That's twice as revolutionary and transcendent as the decision to not use a photorealistic look for the animation" (Remezcla). At school, his teacher asks him to write a personal essay about what kind of person he wants to be. Although writing the essay soon becomes the least of his worries, Miles's journey of discovering who he is and who he aspires to be drives the film forward.

Although speaking of Guillermo Del Toro's films, Iván Eusebio Aguirre Darancou's argument is particularly resonant: "The child characters are thus mobilized not as disempowered social subjects who experience horror, trauma, and violence. . . . In this way, children become active builders of new social orders, able to address the bleak realities of our contemporary moment that adults fear to face" (408). Much like the Spider-Man figures before him, Miles Morales struggles to build a new social order that provides a safe and equitable community for his fellow New Yorkers. Notably, Morales gets help along the way from a host of Spider-Mans who have come before him—Peter Parker, Gwen Stacy, Peni Parker (SP//dr), Peter Porker (Spider-Ham), and Spider-Man Noir. Yet, despite his youth and rookie status, Morales is the one who must lead them as they defeat Doctor Octopus and her team of supervillain cronies, namely Kingpin and Prowler. The world quite literally relies on an Afro-Latino teen to save the day.

Through the highs and lows of becoming Spider-Man and the tremendous responsibilities that come with the title, Miles Morales helps young Latinxs see themselves and understand their own value. Film critic Kayla Sutton states: "Miles exists in a world where he has to choose to either live a normal life or 'wear the mask,' but he doesn't have to choose to exist as either black or Latinx, he blends all the parts that make him unique and interesting, and this is something that younger Afro-Latinx viewers will take away from the film" (Remezcla). In the end, *Spider-Man: Into the Spider-Verse* is not just a great superhero film. It's an important piece of U.S. popular culture that tells young Latinxs that anyone, including them, can change the world. Anyone can save the day and be a hero. As Peter Parker tells Miles Morales, "Anyone can wear the mask"—even an Afro-Latinx teen.

## Conclusion

When the 2020 Emmy Nominations were announced in July 2020, notable actor and comedian John Leguizamo stuck his foot in his mouth by lamenting the virtual absence of Latinx nominees, tweeting, "Why can't we Latinx have a piece of the pie? We are the largest ethnic group in America and missing as if we didn't exist!" (@JohnLeguizamo). While Leguizamo is known for his activism and his critical comedy that challenges the history of Latinx stereotyping, seen in his comedy special *Latin History for Morons*, his tweet was immediately criticized as anti-Black. The criticism is warranted, given that 2020 also witnessed a record number of Black nominees, a much-needed, welcome feat during a brutal period marked by the murders of George Floyd, Breonna Taylor, and Ahmaud Aubery that spurred massive Black Lives Matter protests across the country. By refusing to acknowledge the record number of Black nominees and the overall history of Black erasure and exclusion from these coveted categories, Leguizamo missed the larger point his critics made. Unfortunately, Leguizamo's sentiment is not uncommon, as it also suggests that folks cannot be Black and Latinx, as if somehow these identities are mutually exclusive. And if that is the case, characters like Miles Morales and Victor Vargas are erased from the Latinx narrative that Leguizamo was constructing, one that privileges mestizaje and whiteness. The films we have selected in this chapter explore a broad range of adolescent Latinidad that takes as a fact the presence of Afro-Latinidad. While *Real Women Have Curves* traces a Chicana teenager's working-class, feminist awakening— not unlike *Mosquita y Mari's* emphasis on young Chicana queer love—films like *Spider-Man: Into the Spider-Verse*, *Don't Let Me Drown*, and *Raising Victor Vargas* privilege the voices of Afro-Latinx teenagers who are often overlooked and otherwise erased from problematic, limited visions of Latinidad that uphold centuries of anti-Blackness, colorism, and colonial ideologies. We just wish John Leguizamo would understand that, too.

For further viewing:

- *Don't Let Me Drown* (2009, dir. Cruz Angeles)
- *Girlfight* (2000, dir. Karyn Kusama)
- *How the García Girls Spent Their Summer* (2005, dir. Georgina Garcia Riedel)
- *La Mission* (2009, dir. Peter Bratt)
- *McFarland, USA* (2015, dir. Niki Caro)
- *Quinceañera* (2006, dir. Richard Glatzer and Wash Westmoreland)
- *The Sisterhood of the Traveling Pants* (2005, dir. Ken Kwapis).

## Scholarship on Film

Aldama, Frederick Luis, ed. *Latinx Ciné in the Twenty-First Century*. University of Arizona Press, 2019.

Aldama, Frederick Luis, and Christopher González. *Reel Latinxs: Representation in U.S. Film and TV*. University of Arizona Press, 2019.

Beltrán, Mary C. *Latina/o Stars in U.S. Eyes: The Making and Meanings of Film and TV Stardom*. University of Illinois Press, 2009.

Fregoso, Rosa Linda. *The Bronze Screen: Chicana and Chicano Film Culture*. University of Minnesota Press, 1993.

Mendible, Myra, ed. *From Bananas to Buttocks: The Latina Body in Popular Film and Culture*. University of Texas Press, 2007.

Noriega, Chon. *Shot in America: Television, the State, and the Rise of Chicano Cinema*. University of Minnesota Press, 2000.

Rodriguez, Clara, ed. *Latin Looks: Images of Latinas and Latinos in the U.S. Media*. Westview Press, 1997.

"Do you want to be a papi chulo or a papi feo?"

# "I SIGN MYSELF ACROSS THE LINE"

## Latinx Teens on the Page

"When I was growing up Chicana, I never read anything in school by anyone who had a z in their last name. No González, no Jiménez, no Chávez, no López. And I grew to accept this and eventually to stop looking, since no one showed me that indeed such writers existed," says Tiffany Ana López (*Growing Up Chicana/o* 17). Almost thirty years after López's prophetic statement was published in her edited volume, our own university Latinx students tell us virtually the same thing. Whether in California or Texas, our students are surprised when they finally can study Latinx literature, something they didn't necessarily even know existed. By the time students reach us, they have been in the school system for at least twelve years, with year after year being dedicated to the literary canon, which so happens to be overwhelmingly white and male. Growing up in Louisiana, Trevor didn't read a book penned by a Latinx author until his third year of college. As a quiet and nerdy Chicanita, Cristina remembers reading the *Sweet Valley Twins* series with lightning speed, all the time wondering why virtually all of the characters were upper middle class and, well, white.

In addition to mainstay themes of Latinx literature such as family, identity, and immigration, Latinx writers have often been concerned with teenagers and young people. After all, at one time or another we were all teenagers, stuck in that in-between world of childhood and adulthood. So it should not be surprising that the vast, rich field of

Latinx literature presents us with a fair number of adolescent protagonists who push against, challenge, and question the authority of all-knowing adults while demanding a voice for themselves. In fact, texts that we consider canonical Latinx literature feature young people as budding writers, artists, thinkers, and activists. Can we imagine what the Latinx literary scene would look like without characters like *The House on Mango Street*'s Esperanza (1984), *What Night Brings*'s Marci (2003), or *Under the Feet of Jesus*'s Estrella (1995)? But one important point we need to consider is that, while Esperanza, Marci, and Estrella's youthful voices are foundational to Chicanx/Latinx literature, Sandra Cisneros, Carla Trujillo, and Helena María Viramontes never actually intended for their texts to be read as children's/YA literature. Their works we love and cherish are undoubtedly intended for adult readers, despite their young protagonists, and they are routinely taught in college classrooms across the globe.

But what does it mean to be a Latinx writer whose targeted audience is not the know-it-all grownup in front of the college classroom but young people, adolescents in particular? As much as we celebrate authors like Cisneros, Trujillo, and Viramontes, as well we should, it remains an uncomfortable fact that Latinx YA writers seldom receive the same level of critical acclaim as those who write strictly for "adult" audiences. Few Latinx literature scholars routinely study YA texts, much less make them assigned texts in their college classes. As scholars in the fields of Latinx literature, theatre, and cultural studies, we believe adults and teens alike can learn a lot about power, sexuality, gender, voice, and marginalized identities through the study of YA literature. Through a case study of four significant Latinx writers of YA fiction, this chapter explores the themes that their works unveil as they relate to Latinx teenagers on the page and in real life. Encompassing queerness, Afro-Latinidad, friendship, family, and self-exploration, the novels by Elizabeth Acevedo, Gabby Rivera, Benjamin Alire Sáenz, and Adam Silvera confront the simultaneous complexity, joy, frustration, and wonder of being a Latinx teenager.

## Latinx YA Literature: On Representation, Visibility, and Erasure

Although the second decade of the twenty-first century has witnessed the rise of award-winning Latinx YA writers such as Guadalupe

García McCall, Anna-Marie McLemore, Margarita Engle, Rigoberto González, and Meg Medina, to name only a few, Latinx YA literature is not a new field. In the mid- to late 1990s, Gloria Velásquez's *Roosevelt High* YA series was published, and in the first years of the twenty-first century Alex Sánchez released his *Rainbow Boys* series, some of the first queer Latinx YA fiction ever published. In addition, the famed Chicano poet, children's literature author, and eventual U.S. Poet Laureate Juan Felipe Herrera published *Cinnamon Girl: Letters Found Inside a Cereal Box* in 2005, a YA verse novel that has received little critical attention despite being one of the few works of Latinx YA literature that examines the time period of 9/11 from a distinct Latina, adolescent point of view.

Latinx YA writers publish their work within a context of academic scholarship—both within the wider children's literature field and in Latinx literary studies—that has seldom examined YA literature by Latinxs. In benchmark anthologies such as *The Cambridge Companion to Latina/o American Literature* and *The Norton Anthology of Children's Literature*, Latinx writers are not included, or, even when they are the subject of the volume, as in the case of *The Cambridge Companion*, children's and YA literature are not considered. This double exclusion affirms Latinx children's literature scholar Marilisa Jiménez García's assertion that "scholars in Latinx studies rarely consider the position of literature for youth and writers for young audiences in the study of historically oppressed peoples. That is, in ethnic and postcolonial studies, literature for youth, remains, for the most part, marginalized" (115). The erasure of Latinx YA literature as a viable point of inquiry into issues of race, structural inequality, poverty, anti-immigrant sentiment, and anti-Blackness, among other concerns, would suggest that these themes, when geared toward younger readers, must not be "serious." We suggest the exact opposite. To learn about the xenophobic rationale to "repatriate" (a fancy word for *deport*) Mexicans, many of them U.S. citizens, we urge scholars and students to consider Guadalupe García McCall's YA novel, *All the Stars Denied* (2018). Jenny Torres Sánchez's tragic novel, *We Are Not From Here* (2020), tenderly yet critically examines the traumas of unaccompanied Central American minor children who migrate to the United States, a perilous journey, even for those who make it to El Otro Lado. Latinx queer theorists can, and should, read Charles Rice-González's

*Chulito* (2011) alongside José Esteban Muñoz. Even for readers with tastes that delve into fantasy and science fiction, Latinx YA writers such as Daniel José Older, Lilliam Rivera, Alexandra Villasante, Marta Acosta, Tehlor Kay Mejía, and Ann Dávila Cardinal do not disappoint while they explore myth, violence, neocolonialism, and gender, like their counterparts who publish for adults. We especially consider the significance of YA literature as a necessary intervention to undo centuries of structural white supremacy. If children are indeed "the future," as we all too often hear, then shouldn't YA literature be an apt position from which to consider what kind of future we want? As scholar Angel Daniel Matos explains of the importance of YA literature for a wider readership beyond adolescents: "we tend to read this genre of fiction as adults (despite its apparent simplicity and didactic nature) because it allows us to experience childhood and adolescence in a way that we were never allowed to when we were younger" (95). As avid readers of Latinx YA literature, we often reflect on the texts' power to help us as know-it-all adults to place ourselves in our younger students' perspectives. This is how compassion and transformation can take place. When Latinx literary and cultural studies scholars overlook children and adolescents as members of our communities, we miss out on rich dialogues that consider how the damaging effects of white supremacy and colonization impact young people.

But the larger field of children's and YA literary studies equally erases groundbreaking works by Latinx writers. Marilisa Jiménez García correctly asserts that "when it comes to fundamental questions within the overall field of children's literature such as 'Who is 'the child'?' 'What is childhood?' 'What is children's literature?' scholars have mainly drawn on a heritage of Anglo literature to create theory" (114–15). The problematic erasure of Latinx youth as readers and learners either presupposes the universality of white children's experiences or completely ignores how Latinx young people are also concerned with familiar issues like the challenges of growing up, questioning one's surroundings, and belonging, benchmark themes in literature for youth. In scholarly studies like *Contemporary Dystopian Fiction for Young Adults: Brave New Teenagers*; *Reading Like a Girl: Narrative Intimacy in Contemporary American Young Adult Literature*; *The Edinburgh Companion to Children's Literature*; *Power, Voice, and Subjectivity in Literature for Young Readers*; and *Children's*

*Literature: New Approaches*, to name just a few, Latinx YA literature is excluded from critical discussion.

The very recent edited volumes *Voices of Resistance: Interdisciplinary Approaches to Chican@ Children's Literature* (2018) and *Nerds, Goths, Geeks, and Freaks: Outsiders in Chicanx and Latinx Young Adult Literature* (2020) are the first anthologies of essays on Chicanx/Latinx children's and YA literature. In our edited volume, *Nerds*, we especially wanted a book that made front and center the stories of Latinx teen "weirdos" and outsiders, considering that the last ten years have witnessed an explosion of Latinx YA texts with protagonists who are geeky, don Doc Martens on the regular, and prefer reading books over partying. These Latinx teens embrace their outsider identities even as their peers, mainstream culture, and their Latinx communities attempt to squelch their freaky rebellions. In her 2020 book, *ChicaNerds in Chicana Young Adult Literature: Brown and Nerdy*, Cristina explored Chicana YA characters she dubs ChicaNerds for their insistence on uniting the distinct adolescent Chicana, feminist, working-class identity with "nerdy" attributes like intellectual curiosity that are seldom attributed to young women of color. Rather than reproduce popular culture's tendency to mock or malign nerds, these fierce Chicana teenagers flaunt their nerdiness as fabulous displays of Chicana feminist resistance. The important work by Latinx children's literature scholars such as Phillip Serrato, Cristina Rhodes, Marilisa Jiménez García, Domino Pérez, Isabel Millán, Angel Daniel Matos, and Sonia Alejandra Rodríguez has addressed the critical gaps in existing studies, proving that Latinx YA writers deserve their just due.

## To Chubby and Queer Puerto Rican Girls, With Love: Gabby Rivera's *Juliet Takes a Breath*

What do you get when you pair a chubby, Puerto Rican, "baby dyke" "nerdburger" from the Bronx with the vegan, white, hippie author of *Raging Flower: Embracing Your P\*ssy*? Short answer: the brilliance that is Gabby Rivera's debut YA novel, *Juliet Takes a Breath* (2016), a book that Roxane Gay succinctly describes as "fucking outstanding" in her *Goodreads* review (*Goodreads*). Set in 2003, the novel is loosely based on Rivera's own coming-of-age story, evidenced by the "about the author" blurb: "She wants queer brown girls to see themselves everywhere and to be proud of who they are. Gabby was a nerdburger who always wrote in journals, on stray napkins, and even on her sneakers when it was cool to do that" (265). The timeframe is telling, set only two years after 9/11, a period of incredible strife, uncertainty, suspicion, and routine hypersurveillance that in itself mirrors Juliet's own circuitous path to self-love and queer affirmation. The novel is at times laugh-out-loud funny and other times tender as it chronicles nineteen-year-old Juliet Milagros Palante's first summer after college as she interns in the supposed feminist Utopia of Portland, Oregon with the illustrious expert on all things female, Harlowe Brisbane. In a novel that makes lessons on intersectional feminism accessible to adults, teens, and general readers, the book is also equally powerful for its compassionate treatment of a newly out-to-her-Puerto-Rican-family self-described "geek" and "nerdburger" who struggles to vocalize and proclaim her queer Puerto Ricanness amid pressures to be straight (her mother), "less gringa" (her hood), and "less brown" (her white girlfriend). In other words, Juliet is an outsider both within her community and among the white, feminist, lesbian enclave of Harlowe's Pacific Northwest. Juliet makes a lot of mistakes, asks a lot of questions, and admits when she doesn't understand terms like *polyamory* or *cisgender*, making her an incredibly sympathetic, loveable, and all-too-real character. By the end of the novel, Juliet arrives at a hard-won space of self-acceptance and forgiveness, reminding herself in a letter she writes that she must *"Be proud of your inhaler, your cane, your back brace, your acne* [and]. . . . *Love your fat fucking glorious body"* (259, original italics). That is, Juliet must accept that "haters gonna hate" and that all she can do is love all those attributes that make her a wonderful, fabulous Boricua geek—a *Borigeekua*, if you will—her asthma, her queerness, her curiosity, and her body. Casting off the haters to achieve self-love is, at its core, a radical act of queer Latina feminism.

*Juliet Takes a Breath* traces Juliet's growth from an anxious nineteen-year-old—who avoids coming out to her parents until she departs for a summer-long internship in Portland—to a more honest version of herself. This path to a queer, Latina, working-class feminism begins when she sends fangirl mail to the fictional feminist guru Harlowe Brisbane, whose book, *Raging Flower*, serves as her introduction to feminism and lesbianism. At first, Juliet is rather idealistic regarding Harlowe, and the process by which she begins to realize and address Harlowe's elitist, racist brand of white, liberal feminism is gradual. As Juliet initially believes, Portland "had to be a utopia if Harlowe lived there and wrote *Raging Flower* there. It had to be more soul-affirming than the fucking Bronx, right?" (35). Readers will empathize with Juliet's sincere, if a little misguided, belief that fleeing her neighborhood to venture into uncharted territory will be the answer to all of her burning questions on lesbianism and feminism. Although Juliet at first believes that Portland will help her understand herself and arm her with the metaphorical weapons to slay the patriarchy, she eventually learns that the real tools have been within her community and family all along. As Grisel Y. Acosta states, "Juliet loves her family, and they clearly love her, but her feelings of isolation permeate their interactions because she is longing for peers who understand her queerness" (90). Juliet leaves home to learn to love herself so that she can finally proclaim that she is one *"beautiful brown babe"* (258, original italics). The path to righteous Boricua-babe territory is arduous and messy, but ultimately illuminating.

This brimming optimism stems from Juliet's long-held fears of not fitting in and of being seen as a weirdo who is not "really" Puerto Rican. For Juliet, Harlowe's book serves as a lifeline of sorts, a book that teaches her to embrace and proudly proclaim her lesbianism when she struggles to come out to her family. However, Harlowe's call for a "universal sisterhood" erases queer and trans BIPOC, making this union entirely a facade. Not surprisingly, soon after she arrives in Portland she is bombarded with terms with which she is unfamiliar; she associates this overwhelming and confusing moment with feelings of unbelonging within her home neighborhood: "His queer questions brought back memories of Puerto Rican kids asking me if I knew all the words to Big Pun's part on *Twinz (Deep Cover '98)*. . . . Are you Puerto Rican enough, Juliet Palante? Do you know the words? Are you down with us? Or are you just a white girl with brown skin?" (65). Juliet's feelings of unbelonging amid the identity policing of her community are precisely why she gravitates toward Harlowe, believing that she will find a space of acceptance and affirmation within the feminist environment of Portland. The path to navigating these intersecting facets of her life, such as her queerness, working-class Bronx background, and awkward geekiness, however, is one that is facilitated not through Harlowe but through her mother, her Titi Penny, and her queer cousin, Ava. Her cousin sternly yet lovingly warns her to "watch out for those white girls" because "They're down for Harlowe. They're down for each other. They're not down for you, Juliet Palante from the Bronx" (81). Ava's cautionary advice for her eager prima, rooted in their "mad love" for each other, is most vivid near the end of the text when Juliet learns firsthand the limits of Harlowe's affection *and* white women's liberal feminism.

Ava's prophetic moment occurs when Juliet unwittingly serves as a prop for Harlowe to sell her book's supposed appeal to young, queer Latinas. One of Juliet's first major tasks during her internship entails helping Harlowe organize a reading at the famous Portland bookstore, Powell's. When Harlowe is questioned by a queer Black woman on the unrealistic attainment of universal sisterhood without an acknowledgment of white women's unique brand of racism, Harlowe cruelly cites Juliet as an example of the book's power, effectively tokenizing her in the process: "I know someone right now sitting in this room who is a testament to this, someone who isn't white, who grew up in the ghetto, dodging bullets and crackheads, someone who is lesbian and Latina and fought her whole life to make it out of the Bronx alive and to get an education" (178). In Harlowe's attempt to perform inclusivity, she reveals her inability to look beyond her privileged position as a white woman, failing to recognize the harm she has caused Juliet, who is humiliated but correctly interprets Harlowe's racist stereotyping: "had she really just used me to make a point?" (179). As Juliet painfully learns through this cruel act of tokenization, Harlowe's version of feminism excludes queer, Latina subjects, erasing her as a holder of feminist knowledge, much as her Puerto Rican peers relegate her to the periphery of Latinidad because she possesses geeky and nerdy qualities.

Yet Juliet does find a space of radical love and acceptance, not in Harlowe's worshipping grounds as she initially expected, but within the confines of her extended family, who encourage her to look within their community of BIPOC for feminist inspiration: "Maybe I wasn't such a freak, feminist, alien dyke after all. I was part of this deep-ass legacy and history of people fighting to be free" (195). Juliet learns a painful though necessary lesson on erasure and (in)visibility, at last accepting that "the point of being an outsider is to share the perspective and help others grow via one's insight" (Acosta 91). Ava's distinct feminism centers BIPOC, lovingly teaching her traumatized cousin that this legacy of radical activism belongs to her as a queer Latina. There is room for her in that history, in their community. Juliet belongs.

Ultimately, Juliet learns through her community of women family members—her mother, Titi Penny, and Ava—that feminism must not and should not be inseparable from all facets of her life, be it her queerness, her Boricuaness, or her Bronx neighborhood. For feminism to be meaningful for her community of queer BIPOC *and* her family, it needs to speak to their lived experiences, and only then can Juliet breathe in the love of those around her. Significantly, it is within the loving surroundings of her women family members that she at last comes to realize that chubby, cute, asthmatic, and geeky Boricua queers like herself matter. Although she feared rejection from her mother for coming out as queer, her mother's fierce love and affection, combined with her wise beyond-her-years cousin's gentle lessons, provide all the oxygen she needs.

## "I'm where the X is Marked": Elizabeth Acevedo's *The Poet X*

> "I'm where the X is marked,
> I arrived battle ready—"
> "I am the indication,
> I sign myself across the line.
> The X I am
> is an armored dress
> I clothe myself in every morning." (Acevedo 306)

So says sixteen-year-old protagonist Xiomara Batista, "The Poet X," as she recites her poem in a duel of words against her mother, who prays over the supposed wayward daughter who prefers writing poetry to attending Catholic confirmation classes. Altagracia recites, or rather yells, her own verses—the Hail Mary—at Xiomara in the novel's climactic moment, when she discovers her daughter's private journal filled with poems that she believes are nothing but bochinche. By writing poetry that speaks to her reality as an Afro-Dominican American teenager raised by parents who use religion and silence to punish her,

Xiomara has broken the cardinal rule of keeping quiet, of not keeping "las cosas de la casa en la casa." Writing is her shield, her armor, her way of inserting herself into a world that more often than not refuses to see her and renders her invisible.

Elizabeth Acevedo is one of the most luminous of Latinx YA writers, yet it's rather unbelievable that her most-celebrated novel, *The Poet X*, was only published in 2018. Since then, she has gone on to publish *With the Fire on High* (2019) and *Clap When You Land* (2020), texts that privilege the voices of teenage Afro-Latinas. All three of these book covers also prominently display illustrations of Afro-Latinas, a powerful declaration of Afro-Latinidad that refuses erasure. At a time when the Black Lives Matter Movement challenges Latinx people to confront centuries of anti-Blackness, Acevedo's work is all the more necessary. *The Poet X*, written in verse, as is her most recent text, *Clap When You Land*, tells the story of Xiomara Batista as she develops into her poetic voice and identity while simultaneously navigating her often antagonistic relationship with her mother, her father's stern silence, and her loving relationship with her twin brother, Xavier. Her mother's extreme religiosity is by far the biggest obstacle she faces in attempting to compete in a citywide poetry slam that her friends and English teacher, Ms. Galiano, encourage her to attend. Undoubtedly wanting readers to connect Xiomara's *X* with Malcolm X, who changed his name to shed the vestiges of slavery and the enduring legacy of white-supremacist violence, Xiomara's path to becoming The Poet X, her poetry slam name, is paved with tears, confusion, questions, and frustration with her parents' Catholic rigidity, which wants to mold her into the passive, silent daughter. While an *X* may cross something out, for Xiomara claiming the *X* means to claim that side of her that few people witness—her poetic voice. To become The Poet X and embody resilience, resistance, fierceness, and strength, Xiomara has to learn to anchor her poetry in her own brand of scripture, a mode of reinventing herself as a creative force. Rather than use her fists to fight off the incessant catcalls and harassment that mark her body as "dangerous" and in need of discipline, Xiomara learns to take to the pen to write herself into existence, to let *X* mark her rightful spot.

With Acevedo's use of the verse structure in her novel, she joins a prestigious group of Latinx YA writers who have utilized this poetic element to privilege the protagonist's process of developing a unique voice (Herrera, "Seeking Refuge" 196). The verse form highlights Xiomara's efforts to establish a voice of her own that she must cultivate within her home setting and community, both of which attempt to silence her. The verse form solidifies its structural relationship to content. That is, like its experimental nature, the verse structure mirrors the process of Xiomara's creation of her poetic voice as she grapples with her confining, religious upbringing and the racist sexualization of her Afro-Latina body, which she must constantly defend. Her developing body especially becomes a contested site of conflict:

> The other girls call me conceited. Ho. Thot. Fast.
> When your body takes up more room than your voice
> you are always the target of well-aimed rumors,
> which is why I let my knuckles talk for me. (5)

As an Afro-Latina teenager who is routinely subjected to harassment and bullying, Xiomara must constantly claim her right to bodily agency, letting her fists communicate her rightful rage. Her quiet demeanor, the habit of keeping to herself, makes her appear conceited to others, while her body marks her as free terrain for sexist catcalls from the local bodega regulars. Writing becomes a balm to process the traumas of these daily, unwanted acts of racialized, sexualized violence, helping her "make poems from the sharp feelings inside" (53). And it is this process of casting off others' marks placed on her and replacing them with her own X, her own signature voice, that is the heart of Acevedo's beautiful novel.

Rather than being crossed out by racism and sexism, Xiomara reinvents herself through poetry, at the encouragement of her Afro-Latina English teacher, Ms. Galiano, who introduces her to the power of spoken-word poetry. Xiomara is instantly hooked when she listens to a young Black woman's powerful and affirming words: "I feel heard" (76). In the company of her fellow Tuesday afternoon Poetry Club classmates, Xiomara finds a community of young poets of color who nurture her creativity, helping her discover her own brand of scripture that does not erase her existence as an Afro-Latina teen. Poetry offers up salvation to those in need of a healing salve: "Tuesday has become my equivalent / to Mami's Sunday. A prayer circle" (286). In these moments, Acevedo pays homage to her own former teachers who encouraged her as an aspiring poet, not to mention those talented young artists who turn their bodies *and* words into a type of prayer, the only kind of prayer that Xiomara can relate to, not the religious indoctrination of her mother's rigid Catholicism:

> When I look around the church
> and none of the depictions of angels
> or Jesus and Mary, not one of the disciples
> look like me: morenita and big and angry. (59)

While her mother takes comfort in the Bible and mass, Xiomara looks to her journal and her written words to provide a home for her questions; her doubts about the existence of God, who lives within a religious institution that aligns grace with whiteness; and the incredible sadness she experiences over the fraught relationship with her parents, who at first do not understand her desire to be a writer and an artist.

Xiomara's ongoing battles with Altagracia eventually culminate in a showdown, a verbal duel, when her mother discovers her journal, a moment we referenced in the opening to this section. Altagracia's rage over this discovery of her daughter's "forbidden fruit," so to speak, leads her to a desperate, violent act: She burns Xiomara's coveted journal. The flames consume years' worth of love and labor, "And as she recites Scripture / words tumble out of my mouth too, / all of the poems and stanzas I've memorized spill out" (305). In the chapter entitled "Verses," Acevedo links Xiomara's gritos with Altagracia's, yet, rather than unite in a shared maternal language of love, their verses conflict in a raging volley of words that compete for voice and recognition:

> "My name is hard to say,
> and my hands are hard, too.
> I raise them here
> to build the church of myself.
> This X was always an omen."

> > "Santa María, Madre de Dios,
> > ruega por nosotros, pecadores,

ahora y en la hora de nuestra muerte.
Amén."
(306–07)

The structure of the words side by side produces a visually stunning and jarring effect on the reader, and we can practically hear the gritos and smell the fumes that consume Xiomara's prized possession. While Altagracia beseeches the Virgin Mary to intervene on behalf of her "sinful" daughter, Xiomara's poetry serves as her own house of worship, built not by bricks but by her words. In this powerful, highly charged moment, Xiomara refuses to relent, and, while the flames may engulf her written words, her voice will not be extinguished.

But all along Xiomara has wanted nothing more than her mother's acceptance, to include her in this path toward poetic voice. Meeting her mother halfway, Xiomara seeks help from their parish priest, Father Sean, who facilitates much-needed intervention, providing an opening through which mother, father, daughter, and son can heal and come together. And, in a loving if surprising twist of fate, Xiomara shares the poem she will perform at the citywide slam with her parents, to which Altagracia lends an important piece of advice to her daughter: "next time, en voz alta. / Speak up, Xiomara" (350).

Eventually, with her parents' support, Xiomara performs at the poetry slam, her whole family in attendance. Like Juliet Milagros Palante, who arrives at a space of affirmation in the loving community of Latina family members, Xiomara's path likewise leads to a hard-won state of peace, validation, and poetic resilience. Although speaking of another fictional spoken-word artist, scholar Amanda Ellis's analysis of the protagonist Gabi, from Chicana YA writer Isabel Quintero's novel *Gabi, A Girl in Pieces* (2014), is particularly resonant: "the creation of political art, the practice of writing, and the power of performance poetry serve as vital creative outlets" (16). Writing and performing poetry arms Xiomara with life, energy, and creative spirituality that she cannot find anywhere else. Reminiscent of other young Latinas who yearn to write and create art, such as Esperanza from *The House on Mango Street* (1983) and Julia from *I Am Not Your Perfect Mexican Daughter* (2017), Xiomara declares herself a poet, at last achieving support from her family. But, unlike Esperanza and Julia, Xiomara is not Chicana; she is Afro-Latina and a poet, a young girl we seldom see represented in popular culture or in the written word. Elizabeth Acevedo corrects that erasure. In her beautiful novel, Acevedo speaks to the unheard and silenced young Afro-Latinas through Xiomara, a teenager whose dreams of poetry are threatened. Xiomara does indeed learn to "speak up," using the power of words to declare herself on the page and on the slam stage. The $X$ is her signature, marking her presence wherever she goes.

## On Queer Teen Love and Chicanx Masculinity: Benjamin Alire Sáenz's *Aristotle and Dante Discover the Secrets of the Universe*

In a tweet dated July 24, 2020, Benjamin Alire Sáenz had this to say of his beautiful 2012 novel, *Aristotle and Dante Discover the Secrets of the Universe*: "Ari & Dante came from a silent space that lives inside of me, an aging man. I wrote & I was a boy in love again. Two boys climbed out of my wounded heart—and now they belong more to my readers than they belong to me. It makes me sad and makes me happy too." While this tweet may at first be read as a simple message of gratitude to his readers, it takes on greater importance when we remember that Sáenz did not come out as gay until well into middle age. His age when he came out is further complicated by his brief service as a Catholic priest. As Angel Daniel Matos notes, "Sáenz envisioned *Aristotle and Dante* as a text that was designed to heal both himself and his readership. It is a fictional text written with the partial purpose of helping him to sort out years of self-negation, and even more so, helping him to imagine a queer adolescence that was in many ways inaccessible to him" ("A Narrative" 33). By the time he began publishing YA texts, Sáenz had long been a celebrated author of adult fiction and poetry, such as *Everything Begins and Ends at the Kentucky Club* (2012) and *Carry Me Like Water* (1995). When we consider his prolific record of YA publishing in the mid- to late 2000s, a period marked by his coming-out process, his tweets become all the more laden with the significance of his personal journey of articulating queerness not in his youth, as many of his YA characters, but later in life. Even as a middle-aged, queer Chicano writer, his Chicanx adolescent characters teach him, and by extension us, what it means to be openly queer when it is still not entirely safe to do so. As Matos poignantly reminds us:

The LGBTQ individuals depicted in this genre of fiction have their first kisses and sexual experiences as teens, they go out on dates, they hold hands in public, they come out to their parents, and they actively perform their oppressive high school environments into spaces of liberation and freedom. Most readers of this fiction in their mid-twenties or older were rarely given the chance to experience these things until a much later period in their lives. In other words, it can be argued that many older readers of gay young adult fiction (such as myself) tend to live vicariously through the lives and the actions of the characters in these texts. ("The Conversion" 95-6)

Matos's crucial words recall why youth literature is so relevant for adults like us, who are decades removed from adolescence. Clearly, Sáenz creates characters for his younger self, allowing himself the creative possibilities of imagining a life he was never able to live as a teen. As readers, we are transported to a period in our lives that we can only imagine on the pages before us, but, through these characters and stories, we can envision a better future, a kinder one, for the adolescents we teach and who teach us. For queer Latinx teens, Sáenz's works are a lifeline.

While not his first book of YA fiction, *Aristotle and Dante Discover the Secrets of the Universe* is easily his most well-known and most-studied text by scholars of YA literature. With its prestigious awards, including the Pen/Faulkner, Stonewall Book Award, Pura Belpré, and Lambda Literary Award, it ranks as one of the most highly celebrated works of YA literature, a significant feat when we consider the dismal publishing numbers we cited in the introduction to this book. In this important novel, Sáenz grapples with the struggles of compulsory heterosexuality, gender, adolescent masculinity, and family relationships to chronicle the queer relationship between two young Chicano teens in the 1980s who have vastly different processes of coming out.

In what is especially telling of the novel's efforts to provide a healing and liberating model of Latinx youth queerness, the book's dedication reads: "To all the boys who've had to learn to play by different rules." From the beginning, Sáenz draws attention to how his book pushes against the marginalization that queer boys have historically faced in Chicanx YA literature. The novel reveals the cultural expectations—and restrictions—that influence who and how an adolescent Mexican American boy should be. At the onset of the novel, Aristotle, one of the two protagonists, tells us, "The problem with my life was that it was someone else's idea" (Sáenz 8). Ari is referring to the social expectations and how, as Sáenz reveals later in the novel, much of the adolescent experience is dictated by obligatory gender and sexual roles that our communities impose upon us. As Carolina Alonso argues, the novel is equally significant for how it "problematize[s] the heteronormativity set as the norm in the canonical novels published after the Chicano Movement" (170). Within the parameters of Chicano nationalism, to be Chicano meant to be male, narrowly ascribed as cisgender and heterosexual. Queerness—even the possibility that Chican*as* are part of the Nation as well—was negated. Accordingly, the novel questions these very sociocultural ideals by foregrounding a story of queer self-discovery in Latinx YA fiction, which at the time of the novel's publication was still a rarity aside from representative novels by Rigoberto González, Alex Sánchez, Charles Rice-González, and Gloria Velásquez. As such, the novel presented a counter-narrative that paved the way for a groundswell of queer Latinx YA fiction in the second decade of the twenty-first century.

Sáenz's novel reveals how the mainstream imposes heterosexuality upon young people. That is, from birth, children are expected simply to be straight, and anything beyond that disrupts the system. Whether it is how we expect boys to like blue, sports, superheroes, and roughhousing and girls to like pink, dolls, cooking, and dancing, so much of the adolescent experience is marked by what our communities expect of us. This was especially the case in the late 1980s during which the novel is set. While the novel largely disregards the struggle of queer Latinxs during the 80s, even going so far as to not mention the AIDS epidemic at all, Sáenz does imagine a world in which Chicanx boys can be different. Although we could certainly critique Sáenz's choices regarding the time period, we are not here to do that. Instead, we draw attention to how the novel privileges the voices of two queer Chicanx teen boys who dare to love each other during a time of rampant homophobia and overall erasure of queer teens of color from the few, mainly older, white-dominant scripts of queerness that were available in the 1980s.

The notion of "compulsory heterosexuality" harkens back to feminist theorist Adrienne Rich's foundational essay, "Compulsory Heterosexuality and Lesbian Existence," in which she argues that heterosexuality should be recognized as a political institution, an institution that has excluded queer voices (233–39). Society just expects that boys are straight, and anything beyond that deviates from the norm. This is precisely where Aristotle and Dante enter the picture. They both struggle with their sexuality to varying degrees. Dante quickly comes to understand his queerness even if he does struggle with the awareness that queerness may invite real danger and violence, whereas Ari pushes against it through the novel, not coming to accept his sexuality until the novel's climactic finish. Throughout the book, both boys struggle to accept themselves while also balancing the demands of being Mexican American teenage boys. For instance, when Dante expresses his love for Ari, Ari's response speaks to society's expectations (and demands). If he has learned anything growing up, it's that being queer is taboo. Sáenz writes:

"I love swimming—and you."
I didn't say anything.
"Swimming and you, Ari. Those are the things I love the most."
"You shouldn't say that," I said. (150–51)

Boys aren't allowed to love boys in this universe. And even though Dante frankly doesn't care about expressing his love for Ari, Ari just isn't ready to hear it. After all, straying from the path set out for us leads to trouble.

The novel's middle section, "Letters on a Page," is critical for understanding the process of learning to identify oneself authentically as a queer person and, eventually, come out of the closet if that is a viable and safe option. In this section, the narrative focuses on Ari because Dante moves to Chicago for the year. To address this, Sáenz incorporates the epistolary form to include letters that Dante writes to Ari in which he reveals how he has been experimenting with his sexuality, ultimately coming to terms with the fact that he is gay. Nevertheless, although Dante is confident in his sexuality, he still feels remorse and shame for being queer in a heteronormative society. Dante writes:

*And I keep wondering what they're going to say when I tell them that someday I want to marry a boy. I wonder how that's going to go over? I'm the only son. What's going to happen with the grandchildren thing? I hate that I'm going to disappoint them, Ari. I know I've disappointed you too.* (227)

Dante doesn't want to lie anymore to those whom he loves—his parents and Ari. Even so, Ari is the first person who reassures him that he should live his truth. When Dante thinks that he has disappointed Ari, Ari corrects him: "You haven't disappointed me, Dante" (Sáenz 252). Ari doesn't care about Dante's sexuality; what he cares about is their friendship and growing relationship. Significantly, though, Ari only believes that queerness is an option for Dante. He may not be "disappointed" with Dante, but he is still unable to articulate queerness for himself.

As free as Dante feels, Ari couldn't be more different. He feels the pressure to live up to society's expectations. These limitations, of course, frustrate Ari. He isn't ready to accept the destiny that someone else has set for him: "I didn't think it was my job to accept what everyone said I was and who I should be" (Sáenz 92). These cultural and gender norms block him from seeing who he truly is. As Ari frequently says, "I don't know who I am" (Sáenz 149). This confusion over who he is versus what others want him to be is compounded by the models of Chicano masculinity available to him beyond Dante: his father and his absent brother, Bernardo. Throughout most of the text, Ari's father is depicted as a silent, brooding man who struggles with PTSD as a result of his service in Vietnam. As much as Ari loves his father, he wants more from this relationship. He especially wants his father to divulge the secrets of his older brother's absence from their lives. Bernardo, we learn, is in prison, and for most of the text readers simply know that he's serving a lengthy sentence, but we have no idea, and neither does Ari, of the circumstances surrounding Bernardo's incarceration. Bernardo's simultaneous absence but lingering presence in Ari's consciousness leads to an almost obsessive quest to dig into the secrets that his parents initially refuse to disclose, until finally his mother explains that Bernardo killed a transgender woman sex worker. Ari's proximity to violent masculinity and transphobia complicates his own process of coming out as queer, but his father later provides a loving, transformative possibility for him. Matos argues that the novel "presents readers with a case in which family, and, more specifically, la familia, serves as a conduit for, rather than an obstruction to, a child's emerging queerness" ("A Narrative" 42). This important element is particularly resonant for how it confronts age-old myths of all Chicanx families being unaccepting of queerness. It isn't until the end of the novel that he feels authentic and comfortable living his truth. At the end of the novel his father tells him, "Ari, the problem isn't just that Dante's in love with you. The real problem—for you, anyway—is that you're in love with him" (Sáenz 348). His parents speak truth to what Ari has kept hidden throughout the novel. In particular, Ari's father is positioned as the person who encourages his son to speak his truth, as Matos notes: "In a move that is unusual in representations of Latinx parental figures (especially fathers) in queer YA literature, it is Ari's father who pushes him to come to terms with his latent queerness" ("A Narrative" 44). Although throughout most of the novel his father appears distant, this moment is as revealing for the reader as for Ari himself. Now is the moment in which Ari begins to feel the shame of being queer: "I'm so ashamed. . . . I'm a guy. He's a guy. It's not the way things are supposed to be" (Sáenz 349). Although he admits his love for Dante, it's just not the path he saw for himself. This moment of self-understanding is, naturally, liberating; he finally declares, "I was free" (Sáenz 359). It isn't surprising that this is the first time he has felt free in his life. At the beginning of the novel, Dante is the one who makes Ari feel visible: "What mattered is that Dante's voice felt real. *And I felt real*" (Sáenz 31, original italics). Now, with Dante's love intact and his parents' support, Ari is ready to reject society's heteronormative expectations and embrace his authentic self.

### Latino Bisexuality and Boyhood: *They Both Die at the End* by Adam Silvera

Despite the growing corpus of Latinx YA literature focusing on queer boys, there is still one identity that remains almost entirely excluded from the narrative: bisexual Latinx teens. Bisexuals comprise more than half of the LGB community, and more than 40% of bisexuals also identify as people of color (Gates; Human Rights Campaign). Despite these large numbers, in nearly every facet of U.S. popular culture, bisexual teens face challenges regarding representation. Bisexuals in film and on television are few and far between. More specifically, it's no secret that bisexuality is underrepresented in YA fiction, and, whereas there is a growing corpus of YA lit focusing on bisexual girls, there is a noticeable absence of books written about bisexual boys of any race or ethnicity. As Bonnie Kneen highlights, "The absence of bisexuality in YA fiction thus follows (and reinforces) a broader invisibility that is likely to shape most teenagers' lived experience of bisexuality" (363).

Ultimately, these facts led us to question—where are the stories about bisexual Latino teens? If bisexuality is truly to achieve mainstream visibility, then YA literature must become responsive to this systemic lack of representation. And part of this responsiveness is creating an ecosystem that supports a plurality of bisexual identities that stretch across markers of race and ethnicity. This is to say, Latinx teens rarely get the chance to be bisexual on YA pages. Despite bisexuals comprising the largest demographic of the LGBT community in tandem with the United States' growing Latinx population, there are only a handful of instances of Latino bisexuality in YA literature. Latinx YA novels such as *Boyfriends with Girlfriends* (2011) by Alex Sánchez; *Lucky* (2004) by Eddie de Oliveira; *Dragonlinked: Dragonlinked Chronicles, Volume 1* (2013) and *The Bond: Dragonlinked Chronicles Volume 2* (2014) by Adolfo Garza Jr.; and *They Both Die At the End* (2017), *Infinity Son* (2020), and *Infinity Reaper* (2021) by Adam Silvera remain part of only a handful of books that write Latino teen bisexuality into the narrative.

Although all of the aforementioned novels merit our attention, we turn our attention to Adam Silvera's 2017 novel, *They Both Die At the End*, to explore how the novel pushes against bisexual erasure in Latinx YA fiction while also presenting a blueprint for how Latinx bisexuality might become more visible in U.S. popular culture. Bisexuality is the norm in Silvera's novel. While this might seem inconsequential, as the aforementioned research and statistics indicate, the mere act of writing Latinx bisexuality into the narrative remains a radical—and powerful—act of inclusion. Novels that do so push against the mainstream erasure of bisexuality that is all too common.

The intricate and subtle ways that *They Both Die At the End* writes bisexuality into the narrative render the book singular. At this moment in time, there simply isn't another piece of Latinx literature that does what this book does.

Born in 1990 and raised in the Bronx, Nuyorican writer Adam Silvera has burst onto the scene as a veritable force in the field of YA literature. He has achieved something rare in YA publishing—writing queer Latinx stories that routinely make the *New York Times* Best Seller list. And these aren't watered-down depictions of Latinidad or queerness. His novels *More Happy Than Not* (2015), *History Is All You Left Me* (2017), *What If It's Us* (2018, co-authored with Becky Albertalli), and the *Infinity Cycle* series (*Infinity Son*, 2020; *Infinity Reaper*, 2021) all draw upon Silvera's own positionality as a gay Latino while offering nuanced portrayals of characters who have largely been excluded from the YA canon.

*They Both Die At the End* takes place in what looks and feels just like present-day New York City. But something is different. In this alternate universe, Silvera paints a dystopian world in which people receive a phone call from Death-Cast on the day they are going to die, giving them anywhere from a few seconds to nearly twenty-four hours to live. The phone call doesn't give any details— it just tells them that they are going to die. At the start of the book we meet the two protagonists as it tells the story of Mateo, an eighteen-year-old, gay Puerto Rican homebody, and Rufus, a seventeen-year-old, bisexual Cuban American who has faced many of life's challenges in recent years, including becoming a foster kid after he witnessed his family die. These two teenage boys are going to die, and there is nothing they can do to stop it. Silvera's novel doesn't rely on a single narrator; rather, the point of view frequently flips back and forth between Mateo and Rufus in addition to vignettes from other supporting characters. While some of these brief interludes from other characters may seem unnecessary at first, all of the stories converge at some point, influencing Mateo and Rufus's narrative. Once Mateo and Rufus get the infamous call, they become known as "Deckers," join a social media app called "Last Friend," meet each other, and eventually spend their last day filled with the highs and lows that one would expect from such a story. They process grief, imagine what could have been, make peace with the past, check items off their bucket lists, and fall in love. Oh, and they both die at the end.

While this might seem like a depressing story—after all, it is about two teenagers who are about to die—it is more so a book that celebrates the reasons we live. We live for the people we love. We live for the experiences we get to have. As Mateo and Rufus come to learn, their Death Day is truly about embracing popular sayings such as "carpe diem," "YOLO" (you only live once), and "no day but today," to borrow from the musical *Rent*. Their final day on Earth is about living their lives to the fullest extent, and, as is often the case, it's about doing that with people you love.

*They Both Die At the End* is noteworthy for the ways that Silvera allows bisexuality to be spoken. Whereas Mateo's queerness is never explicitly addressed or given a name—he never says he is gay—Rufus's bisexuality is frequently presented in a very matter-of-fact way. Moreover, Mateo spends his Last Day coming to terms with being gay, which is a radically different experience compared to Rufus, who has accepted this integral part of his Latinidad.

Rufus's narrative begins in an unexpected way. When we meet him, he is jumping his ex-girlfriend's new boyfriend, Peck. He is surrounded by the "Plutos," who at first appear to be a gang but in reality are anything but that—they are a group of teens who live at the same foster home and have become a chosen family. Silvera initially paints Rufus as a stereotypical (straight) cholo before unraveling the character's identity in such a way as to create something entirely original. In fact, Rufus's bisexuality would likely be shocking to a reader who entered the text without any previous knowledge. Yet it is in the initial depiction of the stereotype that reveals the complexities of identity and how, more often than not, youth identities can't fit neatly into a box. They are nuanced and full of contradictions.

Silvera pushes against this binary through Rufus's openness and outness. Indeed, in this moment Rufus is confident in his sexuality; he puts himself out there in such a way as to reject the notion that bisexual males must be in the closet or on the down low. Yes, he admits to having made mistakes, but he's not making them anymore. His Last Day will be done the right way, as an out, bisexual, Cuban American teen.

In contrast to Mateo's struggles with coming to terms with his gayness, Rufus's coming-out is very matter-of-fact and something he feels he *has* to do once his parents and sister get the call from Death Cast telling them they will die within twenty-four hours. After Rufus casually mentions that his sister was the first person he came out to, Mateo asks if he ever came out to his parents:

> "On our last day together, yeah. I couldn't put it off any longer." My parents had never hugged me like they did on their End Day. I'm really proud I spoke up to get that moment out of them. "My mom got really sad because she'd never get a chance to meet her future daughter- or son-in-law." (Silvera 176)

Admittedly, coming out to one's parents on their Last Day is not a normal situation, even in the alternate universe that Silvera's novel constructs. Perhaps knowing that you will never see your child again influences the queer rite of passage. Even so, much like in *Aristotle and Dante Discover the Secrets of the Universe*, Silvera flips the trope of Latinx parents being unaccepting of queerness with the love that Rufus is met with after coming out. In this instance, the only thing that matters to his parents is supporting their child and ensuring that he knows they loved him for who he truly was.

Silvera's *They Both Die At the End* imagines a new normal. It envisions a new world in which queerness is not frowned upon or something that should be hidden. It doesn't have to be worked through or figured out. It simply is. It just exists. That Silvera paints the rules of this world through a bisexual character is all the more noteworthy. It is bisexual Rufus who provides gay Mateo with a roadmap to understand and accept his sexuality. Gone is the trope of the bisexual teen realizing they are different and working through their sexuality before ultimately realizing that it's okay to be bisexual. It's normal.

## Conclusion

As avid readers, one of the things we talk about the most during our epic conversations is how deeply we wish the books we love and study had been available to us when we were teenagers, a period when we most desperately could have used them in our lives. Many of our Latinx students express similar sentiments, often commenting that, if they had read Latinx YA literature as teens, perhaps they would have felt less alone. Maybe less afraid. There was a moment during one of Cristina's classes in March

2020, just days before universities across the country would transition to virtual instruction because of the deadly coronavirus pandemic, that she would remember as one of many examples that demonstrated the power of Latinx literature for young people. After Cristina read *Dreamers* (2018) by Yuyi Morales aloud to her students, one student remarked that she had never had a book read aloud to her, and never one in which the characters were migrants, were brown-skinned, and spoke Spanish. Although already in her twenties, this student was deeply touched by a book that humanized Latinx people, much like her family, and she vowed to buy the book for her younger family members. The novels we discuss in this chapter likewise validate the sometimes-conflicting period of adolescence, a time when we navigate first loves, school, familial pressures, and queerness. Gabby Rivera, Elizabeth Acevedo, Adam Silvera, and Benjamin Alire Sáenz reflect the realities of what it means to be a Latinx teenager, with all the highs, lows, joys, and tragedies that accompany adolescence. This reality may mean coming out as queer when your surroundings don't encourage it. It may mean developing a poetic voice rather than going to confirmation classes. It means seeing yourself on the page and realizing you matter. It means "signing yourself across the line" and discovering the secrets of a vast universe that awaits you.

### For further reading

- Elizabeth Acevedo—*Clap When You Land* (2020), *With the Fire on High* (2019)
- Matt De La Peña—*We Were Here* (2010)
- Rigoberto González—*The Mariposa Club* (2010), *The Mariposa Gown* (2012), *Mariposa U* (2014)
- Anna-Marie McLemore—*Blanca and Roja* (2020), *Dark and Deepest Red* (2020), *The Weight of Feathers* (2015), *When the Moon Was Ours* (2018)
- Isabel Quintero—*Gabi, A Girl in Pieces* (2014)
- Charles Rice-González—*Chulito* (2011)
- Lilliam Rivera—*Dealing in Dreams* (2020), *Never Look Back* (2020), *The Education of Margot Sanchez* (2018)
- Jenny Torres Sánchez—*Because of the Sun* (2017), *Death, Dickinson, and the Demented Life of Frenchie Garcia* (2013), *The Downside of Being Charlie* (2012), *The Fall of Innocence* (2018), *We Are Not from Here* (2020)

Alamillo, Laura, Larissa Mercado-López, and Cristina Herrera, eds. *Voices of Resistance: Interdisciplinary Approaches to Chican@ Children's Literature*. Rowman and Littlefield, 2018.

Boffone, Trevor and Cristina Herrera, eds. *Nerds, Goths, Geeks, and Freaks: Essays on Chicanx and Latinx Young Adult Literature*. Oxford: University Press of Mississippi, 2020.

Boffone, Trevor and Cristina Herrera, eds. "The State of Latinx YA Literature." *Label Me Latina/o*, no. XI (summer 2021): 1–4.

Herrera, Cristina. *ChicaNerds in Chicana Young Adult Literature: Brown and Nerdy*. Routledge, 2020.

Jiménez-García, Marilisa. *Side by Side: US Empire, Puerto Rico, and the Roots of American Youth Literature and Culture*. University Press of Mississippi, 2021.

Matos, Angel Daniel. *The Reparative Possibilities of Queer Young Adult Literature and Culture*. New York: Routledge, 2021.

Rhodes, Cristina. "Corporeal, Phenomenological, and Activist Transformations in Pam Muñoz Ryan's *Esperanza Rising*." *Children's Literature Association Quarterly* 46, no. 1 (spring 2021): 41–56.

Rodriguez, Sonia Alejandra. "'Fierce and Fearless': Dress and Identity in Rigoberto Gonzalez's *The Mariposa Club*." In *MeXicana Fashions: Politics, Self-Adornment, and Identity Construction*, edited by Aida Hurtado and Norma E. Cantu, 216–34. University of Texas Press, 2020.

Serrato, Phillip. "A Portrait of The Artist as a Muchachito: Juan Felipe Herrera's *Downtown Boy* as a Poetic Springboard into Critical Masculinity Studies." In *Voices of Resistance: Interdisciplinary Approaches to Chican@ Children's Literature*, edited by Laura Alamillo, Larissa M. Mercado-Lopez, and Cristina Herrera, 61–76. Rowman and Littlefield, 2018.

## 4

# "I'M ONLY NINETEEN BUT MY MIND IS OLDER"

## Latinx Teens on Stage

In the second act of Lin-Manuel Miranda's ultrapopular Broadway musical *Hamilton* (2015), the audience meets Phillip Hamilton, the son of founding father Alexander Hamilton. In this remix of U.S. history, Phillip Hamilton, originally played by Anthony Ramos, is a definitively Latinx teen whose character arc is pivotal to the musical's plot. When we meet Phillip, he struggles to learn how to play the piano and speak French, but there is one thing he certainly doesn't struggle with—spitting rhymes. As the son of Lin-Manuel Miranda's Alexander Hamilton, Phillip embodies the influence of Latinx rappers on hip-hop culture and, coincidentally, how young people were at the forefront of the hip-hop movement. Rapping gives him confidence, and as he tells us, "I'm only nineteen but my mind is older." As Phillip grows up, he desperately tries to emulate his father, even dying after being shot in a duel that he provoked because someone slandered his father. After Hamilton has an affair with Mariah Reynolds and publishes the details in the ill-fated *Reynolds Pamphlet*, it creates a schism between him and his wife, Eliza. It isn't until Phillip's untimely death that Eliza is able to forgive Alexander. While *Hamilton* is first and foremost about Alexander Hamilton and Aaron Burr, Phillip's narrative presents the significant role that Latinx youth identities play in the American theatre, both on Broadway and on regional theatre stages across the country.

Latinx teens have become essential to not only Latinx theatre but to mainstream American theatre in the United States. Since the advent of the Latinx theatre movement with the activist work of El Teatro Campesino and the Puerto Rican Traveling Theatre in the 1960s, Latinx theatre-makers have routinely dramatized teenage identities and experiences. Admittedly, these works perhaps were sparse in the first few decades of the movement, but the twenty-first century has been a veritable playground for Latinx teens to see themselves represented in multifaceted ways on stages across the United States.

Latinx Theatre for Young Audiences (TYA) is a common site for Latinx teenagers on stage, considering that a "Latinx TYA play authentically centers around the lives and experiences of Latinx youth" (Esquivel). By any account, Latinx TYA has been leading the charge in doing this work since at least the 1970s and 80s, when regional theatres such as Minneapolis' Children's Theatre Company, Seattle Children's Theatre, and Dallas Children's Theatre were founded. In the 1990s, the John F. Kennedy Center for the Performing Arts' New Visions/New Voices festival developed countless new Latinx TYA plays by playwrights such as Silvia González S., Lynne Alvarez, José Cruz González, and Luis Alfaro. Notably, these playwrights had previously written for adult audiences, which in turn led to a more sophisticated theatre than most casual observers of theatre about young people might imagine. The same can be said about canonical Latinx plays about young Latinxs such as *Zoot Suit* (1979) by Luis Valdez and *Simply María, or the American Dream* (1987) by Josefina López.

Despite the growth of Latinx TYA focused on teenagers in recent decades, this chapter instead explores teen identities as they manifest in musicals and plays for adult audiences that have been performed on non-Latinx stages. The case studies in this chapter are all works of theatre that have been able to penetrate the mainstream. That is, these plays have not been relegated to culturally specific Latinx theatre companies. Rather, these works have been produced on Broadway, Off-Broadway, and at major U.S. regional theatres. As such, works like *In the Heights* (2008), *Swimming While Drowning* (2016), *I Am Not Your Perfect Mexican Daughter* (2020), and *Our Dear Dead Drug Lord* (2019) have placed Latinx teens in spaces that have enabled them to further influence U.S. popular culture while also doing important work to expand notions of Latinidad at large. The success of these plays reveals the growing interest that the general public has in seeing Latinxs onstage as well as the desire that Latinx communities have to see themselves represented in legitimate theatre spaces. Yet, as this chapter argues, theatre is able to do something that literature, film, and television simply cannot do—it requires audiences to bear witness to live bodies in the flesh. That is, these Latinx teens are not just characters in a book or a TV show. Rather, they are living, breathing people who share space with audiences. Live theatre performance, therefore, offers countless possibilities to humanize the Latinx teen experience and, as a result, provokes social change.

## Latinx Theatre: 2000–2020

In January 2019, Latinx theatre artists, advocates, and scholars gathered in Austin, Texas for the Latinx Theatre Commons Sin Fronteras Festival and Convening, a four-day-long celebration of Latinx theatre for young audiences co-produced by Roxanne Schroeder-Arce, Emily Aguilar, and Mario Ramirez. Hundreds of festival conveners from across the Americas came to Austin to experience theatre with thousands of young people and to consider the needs and incredible capacities of Latinx audiences of the future. As one festival-goer stated during the closing ceremonies, "sueña con ellos." Dream with them. This festival was precisely that—a chance to dream of what could be. And that world is precisely the one in which Latinx stories are readily available for Latinx teens to bear witness to onstage. Some of these portrayals are TYA, and others are found outside of TYA in plays geared toward general audiences. While the festival offered many glimpses into the power of Latinx theatre, perhaps the best example occurred during a student matinee, which saw hundreds of bilingual Latinx teens watching performer Daniel Loya's Spanish-language solo show *Coatlicue 2.0: La diosa que vino del aire* from Trazmallo Ixinti Company, Mexico City. As the teens entered the theatre, they spoke in English to each other. Immediately following the performance, nearly all students spoke Spanish to each other as they exited the space and returned to their school.

Indeed, there is power in representation, and, as this vignette from Sin Fronteras reveals, seeing Latinx representation on stage affects how Latinx teens perform and experience their identities. By simply witnessing a piece of theatre, these teens completely shifted the way that they interacted with each other, privileging their Spanish-speaking abilities where they once relied on English to communicate with each other. Latinx theatre scholars such as Jorge Huerta, Alberto Sandoval-Sánchez, Nancy Saporta Sternbach, Tiffany Ana López, Teresa Marrero, Cecilia Aragón, Christina Marín, and Roxanne Schroeder-Arce have long focused on the importance of representation considering that seeing Latinx stories onstage can be a transformative experience for young Latinxs and, in particular, teenagers who are in the thick of coming-of-age. Even so, an obstacle remains in not only getting Latinx plays produced but also filling the theatre with young people so that social change can materialize. As Roxanne Schroeder-Arce recognizes, "Latinx theatre created specifically for children and families is in no way new, but it is underrepresented in many communities across the United States" ("Sin Fronteras"). That is, the work has always been done, even if it has been relegated to the sidelines of mainstream culture. As this chapter demonstrates, Latinx teens will no longer stand in the wings; they are ready to take center stage.

In the foreword to the landmark anthology *Palabras del Cielo: An Exploration of Latina/o Theatre for Young Audiences* (2018), compiled by José Casas and edited by Christina Marín, Latinx theatre scholar Jorge Huerta notes:

> Always, the plays center on familia, with one or more children at the center of the story, negotiating their place in a history that has been elided or denied altogether. Further, like the majority of Latina/o plays written for adult audiences, identity is a central issue: who are we? How and where do we belong? These questions are asked by all children, of course, but to a member for a Latina/o family and community these questions seem even more urgent. (7)

While the family is perhaps the most pervasive theme throughout Latinx theatre history, in the twenty-first century, a growing cohort of Latinx playwrights are penning plays with young Latinx characters and stories. Many of these plays go beyond the nuclear family unit to unravel the complexities of teenage identities. Accordingly, there has been a significant increase in representation of teens of all types within theatre and performance. *Palabras del Cielo* highlights the need for diverse representations of Latinidad on U.S. stages and, in particular, for stories that are relevant to young audiences. Marín asserts:

> Young Latina/os have a right to literature that reflects their heritage without pathologizing their existence as the Other. Indeed, all young people have the right to quality literature through which they can learn about the culture of a population that is increasing exponentially in this country. (70)

In the twenty-first century, there has been an explosion of Latinx playwrights penning nuanced portrayals of teenage Latinxs. Accordingly, this cohort of playwrights is pushing against the most predominant themes of Latinx theatre—such as family and immigration—even if they are still tackling how these same things influence young Latinx lived experiences. That is, contemporary playwrights demonstrate how themes such as gender and sexuality intersect with family, class, citizenship, and immigration.

Not surprisingly, immigration remains a significant theme in Latinx theatre. Latinx plays use immigration, citizenship, and undocumentedness to tease out how these themes affect teenagers. Sometimes the teens are grappling with their own immigration status while other times they are trying to hold the pieces together as their family undergoes the dehumanization of being undocumented in the United States and, in some cases, being deported. For example, Karen Zacarías's *Just Like Us* follows four Latinas in Denver who fight for DACA. Tanya Saracho's *Kita y Fernanda* uses the Texas borderlands as its setting to explore how privilege, class, colorism, and citizenship affect two young Tejana girls. Hilary Bettis's *72 Miles to Go*, Quiara Alegría Hudes's *26 Miles*, Quiara Alegría Hudes and Erin McKeown's *Miss You Like Hell*, and Benjamin Benne's *Alma* all feature teens grappling with the sudden, imminent, or possible deportations of their mothers. While immigration and deportation have always been present in Latinx theatre, these plays explore the themes through a definitive twenty-first-century lens, demonstrating that, while the reality of U.S. Latinxs has improved in many ways, immigration forces still seek to dehumanize this community.

Similar to immigration, family is still a fundamental theme in contemporary Latinx theatre, even if playwrights are offering more diverse dramatizations of Latinx families. For example, legendary playwright Midgalia Cruz's *Miriam's Flowers* presents 16-year-old Miriam Nieves, whose family is dealing with the aftermath of her younger brother being accidentally killed by a train while retrieving a baseball from the tracks. Ren Dara Santiago's *The Siblings Play* follows three teenage siblings who have had to raise each other in their parents' absence. Additionally, playwrights flip the Latinx family unit on its head by staging rebellious daughters who subvert traditional gender roles imposed on Latina girls. Fernanda Coppel's *Chimichangas and Zoloft* tells the story of two rebellious teenagers, Jackie and Penelope, who hatch a plan to bring Jackie's mother back home after she binges on prescription Zoloft and greasy chimichangas. Adrienne Dawes's *Teen Dad* features Abby, a precocious emo-goth Afro-Latina teen who orchestrates a surprise, and very unwelcome, weekend reunion for her mother and her birth father. Hilarity ensues. Mónica Sánchez's *Rubi X: #her too* introduces audiences to Rubi, a fifteen-year-old who rebels against her strict mother; everything her mother says she couldn't do "under my roof" Rubi instead does "on the roof." Anthony Aguilar's *Emma and the Suzies* takes a slightly different route, dramatizing Grandma Emma's journey as she relives her rebellious youth tagging in Boyle Heights, Los Angeles in 1967. The Latina teens who fill the worlds of these plays all do things that would have been unthinkable in plays at the onset of the Latinx theatre movement. Aside from works by writers such as Maria Irene Fornés, Estella Portillo-Trambley, and Cherríe Moraga, complex female characters were few and far between on Latinx stages.

In the same way, queer Latinx teens have historically been marginalized in theatre. While the 1990s did see a marked increase in queer Latinx theatre with writers such as Luis Alfaro, Cherríe Moraga, and Guillermo Reyes leading the charge, their plays were not necessarily focused on queer coming-of-age stories from a definitively teenage perspective. Josh Inocéncio's *Purple Eyes* is a solo show dramatizing Inocéncio's coming-of-age as a gay Austro-Mexican in

Texas set against the backdrop of four generations of machismo in his family. Benjamin Benne's *querencia: an imagined autobiography about forbidden fruits* is a memory play about Milo, a thirteen-year-old Latino who struggles to understand his sexuality. Lily Gonzales's *(trans)formada* introduces audiences to Sam, a queer, trans child of Mexican immigrants living in the Texas Hill Country as they embark on a coming-of-age journey to learn how to express their gender and ultimately come out to their mother. These plays all demonstrate how resilient bonds between teenagers and family members can ease the coming-out and coming-of-age processes. In the end, aforementioned playwrights and dramatists such as Georgina Escobar, Christina "CQ" Quintana, Emilio Rodriguez, and Juliany Tavernas are imagining new worlds in which queerness and Latinidad coalesce in ways that simply weren't possible even a few decades earlier.

Ultimately, these examples of Latinx plays that focus on teenagers just represent the tip of the iceberg. Contemporary playwrights are penning more-nuanced depictions of Latinidad than was possible in the early days of the Latinx theatre movement. Speaking of this, playwright Ramon Esquivel acknowledges,

> All writers want the freedom to tell whichever stories thrill or scare them, and Latinx playwrights are no different. However, as a writer, I do feel the responsibility—no, I seize the opportunity—to center my stories on Latinx characters, regardless of plot or theme. While I write for young audiences, I am mindful of Latinx kids who may be seeing characters like themselves for the first time. I want them to see Latinx children dreaming of becoming astronauts, trolling the internet, playing pranks on their friends, and falling in love with stories rooted in another culture.

Contemporary Latinx plays speak to how complex Latinidad is and how it is quite literally impossible to view Latinxs as a monolithic ethnic group. And, by the same logic, it's impossible to view Latinx teenage experiences using a singular rubric. As the four case studies that follow reveal, there are many ways to be a Latinx teen, and all are worthy of their own story.

## Negotiating the So-called American Dream: *In the Heights*

How many Latinx teenagers can you name from Broadway musicals? Unsurprisingly, this question doesn't offer many responses, but there is one show that defied the odds and told a Latinx story written by Latinx writers on Broadway—*In the Heights*. The show also happens to heavily focus on a Nuyorican teen, Nina Rosario. *In the Heights*, with music and lyrics by Lin-Manuel Miranda and book by Quiara Alegría Hudes, won four 2008 Tony Awards and has become the most recognizable Latinx musical. The musical has become an indisputable part of the musical theatre canon. As a Latinx Broadway musical penned by Latinx authors, *In the Heights* is singular in its trajectory and in how it facilitates conversations about representation on Broadway and in regional theatres. Miranda and Hudes's musical was the first Broadway musical "by, for and about Latino/as with a variety of Latino and Latina characters, played by Latino and Latina actors" (Schroeder-Arce, "Representations" 199). It's full of hope and a celebration of home, all told through a Latinx lens. Not surprisingly, it has become a popular show for high school and college theatre programs, as well.

*In the Heights* portrays three hot summer days in the life of a group of people living in Washington Heights, a predominantly Latinx neighborhood in New York City. At the center of the story is Usnavi, who runs the corner bodega that serves as a focal point of the community. At the top of the show, once Usnavi shoos Graffiti Pete away from the bodega, Usnavi begins his rap, introducing us to the family to which we are about to bear witness: Nina, who returns home after losing her scholarship to Stanford; Benny, Nina's love interest who is not Latino and works for Nina's father; Abuela Claudia, the neighborhood's communal grandmother figure; and several others Latinxs who live on the block. Throughout the musical, these characters present dignified portrayals of Latinx identities, rejecting the stereotypes that the mainstream media so often presents.

Not surprisingly, the Latinx community, in particular teenagers, has seldom seen itself represented on the Broadway stage. When *West Side Story* debuted on Broadway in 1957, it became the first commercial show to prominently feature Latinx actors and characters, even if it did usher in one of the mainstay stereotypes of Latinx teenagers—the gang member. In many ways, the residents of Usnavi's block are the antithesis to the Sharks depicted in *West Side Story*. Accordingly, *In the Heights* pushes against the *West Side Story* effect by presenting a handful of multifaceted Latinxs such as Nina Rosario, one of the musical's two leads. She is a college freshman who carries the generational expectations that her parents have inflicted upon her. Despite still being a teenager, Nina is "the one who made it out" of the barrio and, as such, is the one who can build a better life for her family.

Abuela Claudia introduces the backbone of both Nina's journey and the show at large in "Paciencia y Fe," a song that details the struggles she has faced from growing up poor in Havana, Cuba to immigrating to New York City and becoming the matriarch of the block. Abuela Claudia sings:

> And ay Mamá,
> What do you do when,
> Your dreams come true?
> I've spent my life,
> Inheriting dreams from you. (Miranda and Hudes 63)

Like many immigrants from Latin America, the decision to come to the United States was not in Abuela Claudia's hands. Much of her life was planned by her mother, including the dream of finding success— and more importantly home—in Washington Heights. Nearing the end of her life, Abuela Claudia has already achieved some version of the so-called American Dream. As the song hits its climax, she reveals that she has the winning $96,000 lottery ticket. Instead of excitement, she is at a loss. Her mother could never have prepared her for this; she is in uncharted territory much like many children of immigrants who grow up in the United States and face an entirely different reality than their parents ever could have imagined they would face. Abuela Claudia's message permeates the show's other story lines, in particular Nina's. And ultimately, as she tells everyone, all they need to get by is patience and faith (not to mention each other).

In "Breathe" we meet Nina Rosario, who has just returned to Washington Heights after her freshman year at Stanford University. As the one who has made it out of the neighborhood and is seemingly well on her way to achieving the American Dream that her parents planned for her, Nina struggles with these inherited expectations. She is the neighborhood's success story, which makes it even more difficult for her to tell everyone that she had to drop out when she couldn't keep up with her classes because she was working two jobs to pay for books and living expenses. As she tells Abuela Claudia, her freshman year "felt like ten" (Miranda and Hudes 15). When Usnavi asks her, "did you kick some college ass?" she responds, "I got mine handed to me on a silver platter" (Miranda and Hudes 16–17). Despite having a full scholarship to one of the world's premier universities, her struggles reveal just how complicated it is to find success as a Latina nerd away from her family and support system for the first time in her life. Her parents, Kevin and Camila, left Puerto Rico to escape their parents and pursue their dreams in New York City. Their dream? To provide Nina with the life they never could have. The mere act of going to college is a success in and of itself. So, when Nina returns home, she struggles with being autonomous and living up to her parents' high expectations that she will be "the one who made it out" (Miranda and Hudes 19). As she details in "Breathe," she feels like "the biggest disappointment" who "couldn't hack it" (Miranda and Hudes 17). Ultimately, telling her parents the truth is the hardest thing she has had to do. She doesn't know what to say because she knows the sacrifices her parents have made, and, as a first-generation college student, she knows that her parents don't understand what making it at Stanford looks like. The weight of the inherited dreams that Abuela Claudia details hangs over Nina; she simply doesn't want to disappoint her parents.

Eventually Nina tells her parents the truth, which creates a chasm between both her and her parents as well as between her parents themselves when her father Kevin declares that he will sell the family's taxi company that he has built from scratch without first consulting with his wife. To Kevin, Nina's success in college is *the* most important thing in his life. He would rather give up everything he has if it means that his daughter can return to Stanford and someday graduate. In the end, Kevin and Camila decide to go forward with selling the family business. They've made it work before, and they will make it work again. Their teenage daughter's success is too important to them. More sacrifices will be made, and, most importantly, Nina will indeed be "the one who made it out."

Lin-Manuel Miranda began working on *In the Heights* while he was a sophomore at Wesleyan University in 1999, and it took nearly a decade to premiere on Broadway in 2008 (Hudes would come on as the musical's book writer later in the process). The humanity of the show extends beyond what is seen on stage and is an integral part of the show's ethos and origins. For example, during an early performance for potential investors, Miranda received feedback that the central conflict of the show, namely Nina dropping out of college, was not enough of a high-stakes conflict for a commercial Broadway musical. Investors wanted Nina to struggle with something "bigger" such as drug addiction or teen pregnancy. In other words, investors didn't think the show could be a success unless it relied on stereotypes. Miranda stood firm because Nina struggling with being a first-generation college student *is* high stakes. Stanford University boasts an acceptance rate of 5%, and its student body is around 16% Latinx. For Nina, as a child of Puerto Rican migrants to New York City, merely to be in a place like Stanford is incredibly high stakes already. She doesn't need to be pregnant or turn to alcohol to be relatable to audiences. This Latina teen is already enough.

This is precisely the beauty of *In the Heights*. The show is built in such a way as to present characters from everyday life. Even if someone isn't Latinx or doesn't live in New York City, they will inevitably recognize the world that *In the Heights* portrays. To put it into simple terms, the show is incredibly relatable. And this is particularly true with Nina's journey. As an intellectual Latina teen, we see her struggles to live up to the high expectations her family and community have set for her. In the end, Miranda and Hudes's hit musical sheds light on the power of community and, of course, the power of young Latinxs to be the change they wish to see in the world.

## Gay, Latino, and Homeless: *Swimming While Drowning*

Since graduating from the University of California, Irvine and uprooting himself to Detroit to teach high school for Teach for America in 2011, playwright Emilio Rodriguez has always been dedicated to working with teenagers of color and telling their stories through his writing and theatre-making. Rodriguez "writes from a commitment to address current, real world concerns" (Sanchez Saltveit). His signature play, *Swimming While Drowning*, is no different. With over seven full productions and countless staged readings since its premiere in

2016 at Milagro in Portland, Oregon, *Swimming While Drowning* has quickly become one of the most popular Latinx plays of the past two decades. The play has been produced at culturally specific Latinx theatre companies as well as regional theatres such as Stages in Houston, lending itself to widespread conversations about queer Latinx teens and the issues they face today.

Rodriguez wrote the one-act play after volunteering at an LGBTQ homeless shelter and interviewing several people who had lived in them about their experiences. He noticed one distinct commonality—many homeless, queer youth felt the need to lie about themselves to stay at the shelter since homeless shelters for queer teens seldom have ample space. *Swimming While Drowning* focuses on two gay Latino teens living at a shelter in Los Angeles. Angelo Mendez, a light-skinned Latino, leaves his home out of the fear of not living up to his homophobic father's expectations. At the shelter, his Afro-Latino roommate Mila helps him find his authentic voice. In the end, Angelo learns how to cope with heartbreak through writing and performance.

The play is not plot-driven; rather, it instead is dedicated to character and thematic development. Rodriguez offers a series of vignettes between the two boys that highlights their friendship while also weaving in issues of (un)belonging, race, ethnicity, sexuality, and the ever-increasing familial and societal expectations both Angelo and Mila face. The play pushes against several stereotypes of "Latino urban youth identity, subsequently broadening the identities of young Latinos" (Boffone, "Young, Gay, and Latino" 146). In writing the play, Rodriguez admits, "I also wanted to write authentic teenagers who are flawed and learning just like I was when I was 15" (Boffone, "FAQs"). At its core, *Swimming While Drowning* is about survival. What must each teen do to survive their homelessness, their losses, their youth, and, ultimately, their sexuality? How can Angelo and Mila help each other survive?

Even though queer teens of color certainly face the challenges of racial and ethnic oppression, queer Latinx youth must also contend with many challenges unknown to their straight counterparts, namely issues that largely affect mental health. Queer and questioning teens are at higher risks for depression, drug use, suicide, and school difficulties. For example, several studies show that LGBTQ teens face higher rates of both bullying and suicide attempts in addition to a stronger likelihood of parental rejection and emotional neglect (Boffone, "Young, Gay, Latino" 149–51). Moreover, queer youth are disproportionately affected by homelessness. Even though LGBTQ youth comprise around 7% of the total youth population in the United States, they make up about 40% of the youth homeless population (Durso and Gates 2). Notably, several Latinx playwrights have tackled the subject of teenage homelessness and taking to the streets to make a living. Plays such as Migdalia Cruz's *Salt*, Jose Casas's *somebody's children*, Beto O'Byrne's *You're Not Alone (anymore)*, and Monet Hurst-Mendoza's *Lilia* all comment on how teenage sexuality intersects with the city and politics, effectively revealing how the state holds the potential to harm young people, especially teens of color. In conversation with these works, *Swimming While Drowning* breaks ground not only in dramatizing homeless youth but also in how Rodriguez's play portrays queer Latino boys in a multifaceted way.

Angelo finds himself in the homeless shelter because of neglect and rejection from his family. He claims that his dad beat him when he came out: "He beat the shit out of me until I bled. The neighbors had to call the cops when they heard the screaming. They found me in a pool of my own blood. The best part: My dad made a smiley face out of the blood on the ground" (Rodriguez 24). After Mila is beaten up by a group of guys one night, he seeks comfort and advice from Angelo. He wants to know how Angelo handled the physical abuse from his father. In this moment, Angelo reveals that he was lying—his father never beat him. Angelo explains the pain he felt when he came out to his father: "If you could've seen the look in his eyes. . . . It was worse than a beating. He looked at me like he wished I was never born. . . . He gave me THAT look for sixteen seconds; he sucked the air out of the room. . . . That was no stare. Staring is something *humans* do. *This* was something else. *He* was something else" (Rodriguez 60). Even if Angelo has never suffered physical violence for being gay, his experience speaks to the hardships that emerge from familial relationships for queer youth. Although he was not kicked out of the house, his father's reaction encouraged him to run away and seek housing in a gay homeless shelter. Because space is so limited in the shelter, Angelo lies about having been beaten by his father so that he won't be turned away. Lying becomes a survival tactic. In any case, Angelo can vividly imagine the possibility of violence, which suggests how queer Latinx youth are always potential victims.

Contrary to Angelo's journey, Mila finds himself in the shelter after fleeing a legitimately abusive home situation in which he has been sexually abused by his aunt's boyfriend. This brings him to his current reality. To Mila, living on the streets and in shelters is a more feasible option for living a fulfilled life. His struggles peak when he turns to survival sex, a practice whereby he exchanges sex for money. Driven by financial benefits and the desire to feel self-worth, queer homeless youth sometimes view transactional sex as a viable option for their future. For many, trading sex seems like the only way for money, food, and shelter. In addition to the financial benefits, homeless youth at times partake in the practice to feel valued. When Angelo asks Mila about sex work, Mila tells him, "It is not as bad as you think," because the men he has sex with "talk to him differently" (Rodriguez 51). These men make Mila feel "special" (Rodriguez 51). In this case, Mila does not see himself as a victim. Throughout the play, Mila makes it clear that he does not realize his self-worth; he isolates himself and continually creates barriers for himself and Angelo, seemingly the only person in his life who sees the beauty in Mila.

In *Swimming While Drowning*'s final moments, Mila and Angelo each take the stage alone to tell us how their time in the shelter has influenced them and how they changed each other (even if they likely will never see or hear from each other again). After sneaking out of bed and packing up his belongings in the middle of the night, the lights shift, focusing solely on Mila. "I got the guard of a soldier when he's under attack / You took the rhythm out of me but I don't want it back / Cuz I gotta lotta bags I wanna unpack / Leave the old me behind no more circles on the track" (Rodriguez 85). As Mila's poem reaches its climax, the sound of a bus approaching is heard. The lights shift and he is gone forever. In the near future, Angelo takes the stage of a poetry lounge to perform "Swimming While Drowning," a poem dedicated to love and the longing to reconnect with Mila. As Angelo professes, Mila helped him survive the shelter. "This is not a poem / This is a thank you / To the man who made / The weight of the world / Just a little bit lighter. . . . This is not a poem / This is an ode / To the man who / Took the words inside me / And created a writer" (Rodriguez 87). With Mila gone, Angelo now recognizes how sharing space and intimacy with another gay Latino teen not only enabled him to accept himself but also gave him the confidence to achieve his dream of becoming a writer.

*Swimming While Drowning* portrays Latino boyhood outside of the margins, forging new space in theatre for underrepresented identities to flourish. Yet stories such as Angelo and Mila's—that is, stories about queer Latino boys—often go unnoticed in popular culture. As always, when we bear witness to theatre performance, we must question who is being represented and why certain gaps exist. As Emilio Rodriguez's play reveals, now is the time to recognize homeless, gay Latino teens not only on our stages but, most importantly, in our communities. The intersections of queerness and homelessness remain pressing issues across the United States. To understand contemporary youth cultures and how young people influence popular culture, these issues must be at the forefront.

## To Be a Misfit Chicana Nerd: *I Am Not Your Perfect Mexican Daughter*

Latina nerds are having a moment. Anywhere you look—on stage, on screen, on the written page, in the House of Representatives (hello, Alexandria Ocasio-Cortez!)—Latina nerds are taking up space and offering nuanced depictions of Latinx identities and experiences, something that has all too often been left out of mainstream media. As we have recognized throughout this book, Latinx nerds, in particular Latinas, have cemented their place alongside other classic archetypes of teenage Latinidad. Theatre is no different. Playwrights have placed front and center Latinx nerds and other outsiders, giving valuable representation to a community of nerds who have long been on the margins of—and often stereotypes of—mainstream Latinx identity.

This reality of the Latina nerd finally entering mainstream U.S. popular culture is precisely where Isaac Gómez's stage adaptation of Erika L. Sánchez's best-selling 2017 YA novel *I Am Not Your Perfect Mexican Daughter* intervenes. The play premiered in 2020 at Chicago's famed Steppenwolf Theatre. Although it closed early due to the COVID-19 pandemic, Steppenwolf committed to reviving the production after the pandemic, this time on its mainstage. A Latina teen gracing Steppenwolf's mainstage should not be overlooked. Chicago's population of 2.6 million people is around 28% Latinx, many of whom are young people. In the end, *Mexican Daughter* is not just a Latinx story; it's a Chicago story, too.

In many ways, *Mexican Daughter* is the twenty-first century's answer to Sandra Cisneros's groundbreaking *The House on Mango Street*. The play tells the story of Julia, a high school student in Chicago, who must navigate the ups and downs of following her dream to become a writer. After her older sister, Olga, tragically dies after being hit by a bus, Julia begins to question if her sister was as perfect as she seemed. Throughout her journey, she questions the mysteries that surround her family, inevitably coming to find herself and her place in the world. Julia is forced to face the skeletons in her family's closet if she is to continue her Chicana feminist coming-to-consciousness and aspirations of becoming a poet. In writing the novel, Sánchez admits that Latina teen representation was a driving force: "I wanted to provide this story to young women of color because I think it's important for them to see themselves and to know that they're not alone. That their experiences are important and that they matter" (Prado). Complex portrayals of Latina teens such as Julia are essential. Young audiences, and readers for that matter, must see how messy and nonlinear the coming-of-age experience can be. There is no one-size-fits-all way to be a Latina teen.

Julia is an uber-nerd. She loves school, especially English class. She loves to write and wants to be a poet one day. She dreams of going to college in New York and finding success far away from her family in Chicago. Her story is led by a sense of intellectual curiosity that simply cannot be contained. Julia is a ChicaNerd, a term coined by Cristina Herrera to describe Chicana nerds: "interesting, sometimes quirky, smart, astute young women who exist outside the white mainstream and on the fringes of the Chicanx communities they love *and* critique" (Herrera, *ChicaNerds* 2). Perhaps most significantly, ChicaNerd identities are a "statement of brown girl self-love, seldom visible in popular culture" (Herrera, *ChicaNerds* 2). While the other Latinx nerds in this book develop their nerd identities in unique ways, Julia's nerdiness is a direct result of her unhappiness with her family. At every turn, she feels like an outsider within her own family.

After her sister's unexpected death, Julia struggles to cope with her family's grief and the seemingly unrealistic expectations her mother has set for her. Julia comes from conservative Mexican parents who don't understand her desires to be more than just an obedient wife. Throughout the play, Julia pushes against the notion that she must be the "perfect Mexican daughter." As Julia tells the audience, "I don't know why I've always been like this. Why the smallest things in the world make me ache inside" (Gómez 53). She is cynical, sarcastic, and rebellious seemingly at every turn. And of course, despite how strong she attempts to be on the outside, she is struggling with her identity and place in the world. Responding to this struggle, Julia's ChicaNerd identity "manifests itself as rebellion, even outright rejection of her parents at times, particularly her mother, with whom she argues throughout" (Herrera, *ChicaNerds* 88). She wants to write and go away to college. She wants to be different and be accepted for those differences. As the walls between her and her parents grow higher and higher throughout the play, Julia becomes lonelier and more depressed, leading to the story's climax. Depression creeps in, and Julia attempts suicide, representing the mental health issues that many Latinx teens face. Julia is lonely, which ultimately drives her story forward as she comes of age with writing and literature becoming her most reliable sources of strength.

For Julia, writing becomes a constant source of strength and self-understanding. As Latinx literature scholar Adrianna M. Santos notes in her work on the YA novels *Gabi, a Girl in Pieces* and *I Am Not Your Perfect Mexican Daughter*, "The everyday resistance to patriarchy and sexism with the texts privilege young women's points of view. . . . Their narratives explore the value of writing as an activity of self-making and empowerment" (45–46). By situating writing as a site of agency and self-actualization, Julia transitions from margin to center, effectively becoming the protagonist in her own story. While trying to understand who she is and, perhaps most importantly, who she is meant to be, she uses writing as "not only a means of self-expression but also as a way to both unravel and remake" herself (Santos 46).

In one of the play's most affecting scenes, Julia's mother, Amparo, rips out the pages of Julia's beloved journal. As writing is the thing that Julia holds closest to her heart, this cuts like a knife. Yet Julia comes to learn that Amparo's own act was, in fact, an act of rebellion. During a brief trip to visit her family in Mexico, Julia finds out that her mother was brutally raped while crossing the U.S.–Mexico border. Amparo's strictness has always been a strategy to protect Julia from the things that no one protected her from. Ripping out the pages of Julia's journal is her own way to process grief and rage. Julia ultimately comes to realize what most teenagers never fully grasp—that their parents struggle with many of the same problems that they do.

At the end of the play, Julia's growth is far from over. She now recognizes that she has the love of her family going forward. Her family takes her to the airport and gives her their blessing as she goes to NYU to study writing. This moment of support shows that the play also pushes against the common myth that Latinx parents, especially undocumented ones, don't care about their kids' education. And she understands that her rebellious nerdiness is intrinsically tied to the pain she and her family have experienced. Indeed, identity is confusing. Once on the plane, she sits next to someone who looks just like Olga, is named Olga, and is played by the same actor who plays Olga. This Olga tells Julia that her sister also goes to NYU and loves it. As they settle into the flight, Olga, along with everyone else on the plane, pulls out a copy of Erika Sánchez's novel to read. Even Julia opens a copy of *I Am Not Your Mexican Daughter*. She declares "How amazing is it . . . that I hold a piece of my sister right here in my hands?" and smiles as the lights fade to black (Gómez 132). As Julia can attest, writing can be a source of empowerment. In the end, she is the author of her own story. Julia, like so many nerdy Latinx teens, is resilient.

By situating nerdiness as a critical aspect of Julia's identity, *Mexican Daughter* normalizes Latinx teens who are creative, smart, studious, and politically engaged. Intellectual curiosity and love of learning are, therefore, strategies of resistance that Latinx nerds take on to push against, and inevitably reject, common stereotypes of young Latinxs being "at risk." Accordingly, plays such as *Mexican Daughter* demonstrate how fictional depictions of ChicaNerds such as Julia are acts of Chicana feminism, considering that they push against the stereotypical representations of Chicana teens that have plagued U.S. popular culture.

This is precisely where Gómez's play holds power. While oftentimes depictions of teenagers—especially Latinx ones—can be watered-down versions of reality, the stage adaptation of *Mexican Daughter* hits all the spots. Julia and her friends greet each other by saying "Hey, bitch!" while eating Flamin' Hot Cheetos like they are getting paid for it. These teens curse. They smoke pot. They have sex. They struggle with body image. They don't always like their families, and they do not always live up to their parents' lofty expectations. They battle with depression and suicidal thoughts. And, oh yeah, they do fully choreographed Quinceañera dance routines.

Notably, Steppenwolf's world premiere of *Mexican Daughter* was dedicated to filling the theatre with teenage audiences. Theatre should not just be a luxury that is afforded to those with privilege. Theatres should view young Latinxs as viable audience members, and not only when the play is about a Latinx teenager. Given Chicago's large Latinx population, Latinx teens are not just the future; they are the present. Steppenwolf recognized this. Weekday student matinees reserved for school groups saw around five thousand public school students attend the production. As *Latinx Teens* has demonstrated, a critical aspect of this work is, in fact, ensuring that actual Latinx teens have access to the material. Only then can social change begin to materialize.

## Girls Being Bad: *Our Dear Dead Drug Lord*

"On Wednesdays, we wear pink," affirms Regina George in the 2004 cult classic comedy *Mean Girls*. George, leader of The Plastics, is the Queen Bee, the hottest girl in school, and definitively blonde. Oh, and she's mean. Like really, really mean. And, while Tina Fey's breakout film—and hit Broadway musical—revolves around the world that George has created, it ultimately shies away from any meaningful discussion about race, ethnicity, queerness, drug usage, and politics.

So, what happens when *Mean Girls* meets *Narcos*? What happens when the pervasive whiteness of *Mean Girls* is distorted through a Jewish Latinx intersectional feminist filter and The Plastics become the Dead Leaders Club? When the blonde leader with the perfect body becomes a tough, queer Cuban American teen? Or when the new girl from Africa becomes the mysterious girl whose dad may or may not be famed drug lord Pablo Escobar? While these questions may seem far-fetched, they are precisely where playwright Alexis Scheer grounds *Our Dear Dead Drug Lord*, which premiered Off-Broadway at WP Theater/Second Stage in 2019, extending several times due to high ticket demand. Much like Sarah DeLappe's enormously popular play *The Wolves*, *Our Dear Dead Drug Lord*'s widespread success demonstrates how audiences are hungry for complex stories about teenage girls.

*Our Dear Dead Drug Lord* follows the four members of the Dead Leaders Club, who try, to put it lightly, to exorcise the patriarchy. The four girls—Pipe, Zoom, Kit, and Squeeze—embody the nuances of girlhood and how, sometimes, girls just want to be bad and do the things that society constantly tells them they can't do. At the play's start, they welcome a new member of the club, Kit, the daughter of a single Colombian mother. The other girls, naturally, think she might be Pablo Escobar's daughter. Pipe and Kit's sexual attraction drives much of the play's action. As a satire on teen girls, the play starts light and funny but soon gets serious as the hunt to uncover the truth about Kit and Escobar comes to a screaming climax.

By any account, the play is a raw look at the violence and eroticism of girlhood. Scheer acknowledges, "My mom is [understandably] horrified that I wrote this play" (Boffone, "Alexis Scheer"). Much of these horrifying things are in fact ritualistic for the Dead Leaders Club. Some of these rituals are harmless, involving a ouija board, candles, totems, incantations, and the like. Other rituals are anything but harmless; the club members dabble in alcohol, weed, cocaine, animal sacrifices, and, in perhaps the most shocking moment on stage in recent years, a coat-hanger abortion in the most literal sense. They do all of these things and more in the name of Pablo Escobar.

Rather than look at the present political moment or even imagine the future, Scheer instead swings the pendulum back to comment on the past and how the names and dates may have changed, but the issues ultimately have not. The play heavily focuses on the landmark election of Barack Obama; it is as much a critique of the Trump presidency and the blind support he enjoys from the MAGA cohort as it is a critique of life in Miami when the United States elected its first Black president. Scheer's play is set before and after the 2008 presidential election, an event that informs how each of the four girls experiences their identity, offering parallels between then and now. As the girls frequently comment, the Dead Leaders Club president, Pipe, is a Republican, even though she routinely rejects this label, the John McCain sign in her front yard notwithstanding. As much as she tries to dismiss and rebel against her upbringing, Pipe can't shed the fact that she is an upper-middle-class Cuban American, and while she may critique it, it's something that gives her power, and Pipe *loves* power. Scheer sprinkles little tidbits of nuance such as this on each character, effectively creating fully fledged, multidimensional depictions of contemporary girlhood.

Pipe is the club's undisputed leader. She is a senior, ambitious and ruthless. In an interview with *Playbill*, Carmen Berkeley, who played Pipe in the Off-Broadway production, notes:

> On the outside she looks polished and privileged, but on the inside she's completely lost. What I love is how she slowly reveals herself to the audience throughout the play. For the first five minutes you might think, "oh, she's that girl," but as the play unfolds, she starts to peel back all her layers and step into her true self. (Peikert)

Pipe is the daughter of an influential lawyer. Like her parents, she clings to capital-R Republican ideals, resultant from the Cuban Revolution and the Castro regime. Even as much of what she says and does would appear to contradict her Republicanism, she clings to it because, well, she associates it with power, and Pipe is power hungry.

While the club's focus is undoubtedly on the titular drug lord, Pablo Escobar, their journey is truly about Pipe's need for power and the ways that the club allows her to go unchecked as she becomes a reckless leader. She picks Escobar both to push against the left, which she sees as moralistic, and against the supposed oppression the club has faced at their elite private school, something Pipe claims infringes on their First Amendment rights. Still, even the club's suspension from school is hazy. Kit reminds Pipe, "You guys were suspended cause you spent club money on drugs and you chose a criminal to worship?" (Scheer 7). As Pipe proclaims, it could have been worse: "Well, first it was Hitler, but somebody called us a hate group when we started wearing swastikas to school" (Scheer 7). In this moment, like many in the play, it's quite literally impossible to know if she's joking or not. It isn't even apparent whether Pipe knows.

Every year the Dead Leaders Club picks a new leader, a process that started with John F. Kennedy when the club was originally founded but slowly evolved to speak to our blind worship of leaders. Since the club has been suspended from school, they begin meeting in Pipe's expansive treehouse where their new focus is none other than famed Colombian drug lord Pablo Escobar. The girls learn everything they can about Escobar, even trying to use a ouija board and an internet search for witchcraft to resurrect Escobar's spirit from the grave.

Although the other girls voice concern that the club's practices have gone too far, Pipe keeps her foot on the gas. During one of the more shocking scenes, the girls perform a ritual animal sacrifice to bring back the spirit of Escobar. When Zoom tries to stop Pipe, pleading, "You can't kill it! That would make us, like, psychopaths," Pipe snaps back, "It's a sacrificial offering. It's different" (Scheer 22). As always, Pipe is testing the limits and gauging how much power she can hold over this group. As determined to gain power as Pipe is, the other girls also demonstrate how blind faith in leaders is indeed problematic. As much as the group worships Escobar, the girls venerate Pipe, as well.

In addition to Pablo Escobar, Pipe becomes increasingly fascinated by Kit. Throughout the play, the two build sexual tension. As much as Pipe tries to suppress it, when the two are finally alone, she kisses Kit. She immediately backtracks her actions: "I didn't even realize—I'm *not*—I mean. . . . I don't know—*was* I sending signals? I . . . think I'm attracted to power" (Scheer 45). In this instance, it's clear that Pipe views her queerness as intrinsically tied to power. Since Kit is the supposed daughter of Escobar, getting entangled in a sexual and romantic tryst with her enables Pipe to experience the feeling of power. She isn't really interested in Kit, but she is aroused by what Kit potentially represents.

At the play's climax, the girls (spoiler alert) successfully resurrect Pablo Escobar. Pipe's third eye is opened, and she declares: "i will not be good. / I will be loud. / have things and not be had. / make the world in my image. / and take. what's. mine" (Scheer 97). Pipe embraces her agency and further commits to being the author of her own story. She will no longer be subsidiary to men, or anyone else for that matter. Just like the leaders who have come before her, she will unapologetically take what is hers and, for better or for worse, change the world.

*Our Dear Dead Drug Lord* dramatizes Latina teens gaining and retaining power. They aren't interested in being "sorry" or "good," but they want to sit in their imperfections and strive to amount to something, perhaps even something beyond the physics of the real world.

Scheer's play offers no apologies and pulls no punches in portraying these teens. Audiences are hungry for these stories not only of girlhood but, more importantly, of girls being bad and doing things that society doesn't expect them to do. And while we see them perform witchcraft, do drugs, talk explicitly about sex, and do some other things we'll leave to your imagination, one must wonder why we expect this behavior from boys, but when girls do it it's considered taboo.

The critical and commercial success of *Our Dear Dead Drug Lord*, like its twenty-first-century counterpart, *Mean Girls* (not to mention the 1980s *Heathers*), reveals that we don't just like watching girls being bad—we actually kind of sort of love it.

## Conclusion

On June 15, 2008, Lin-Manuel Miranda drew national attention when he rapped his acceptance speech for the Tony Award for Best Original Score for his work on *In the Heights*. While Miranda became the first person to rap a Tony Award acceptance speech, what captured the attention of his Latinx audiences was his pulling out the Puerto Rican flag, thanking the entire island and its peoples in diaspora. In a way that had been absent since the Sharks graced Broadway in *West Side Story*, Puerto Ricans saw themselves represented on the Great White Way. Not only was a Puerto Rican finding mainstream theatre success, but he also was doing so in a way that did not compromise his Latinidad or Boricua heritage. *In the Heights* became *the* hit of 2008, positioning its lead character Nina Rosario as a Latina teen occupying the most famous theatre space in the world. Following the musical's Tony successes, audiences poured into the Richard Rodgers Theatre for three years to watch Nina and her Washington Heights *familia* realize that what matters most in life is who we do life with. Although Nina is an intellectual Latina that will be the neighborhood's success story, she didn't get there alone. Her success is the community's success. And, as the plays in this chapter reveal, the work of Latinx theatre-makers speaks to how the complex lives of Latinx teenagers are ripe for mainstream theatre spaces across the United States. These are exactly the type of plays that audiences need right now. So, grab yourself a bag of Flamin' Hot Cheetos and be a part of the age of the Latinx teens on stage. The time is now.

For further reading:

* Matt Barbot—*Princess Clara of Loisaida*
* Benjamin Benne—*querencia: an imagined autobiography about forbidden fruits*
* Diana Burbano—*Fabulous Monsters*
* Migdalia Cruz—*The Have-Little*
* Kristoffer Diaz—*Welcome to Arroyo's*
* Noah Diaz—*Richard, Jane, Dick, and Sally*
* Mercedes Floresislas—*Los Moreno*
* Isaac Gómez—*La Ruta*
* Virginia Grise—*blu*
* Alvaro Saar Rios—*Luchadora.*

## Scholarship on Latinx Theatre

Boffone, Trevor, Teresa Marrero, and Chantal Rodriguez. *Encuentro: Latinx Performance for the New American Theatre.* Northwestern University Press, 2019.

Boffone, Trevor, Teresa Marrero, and Chantal Rodriguez. *Seeking Common Ground: Latinx and Latin American Theatre and Performance.* London: Methuen Publishing Company, 2021.

Boffone, Trevor and Carla Della Gatta. *Shakespeare & Latinidad.* Edinburgh University Press, 2021.

Casas, Jose, compiler, and Christina Marin, editor. *Palabras del Cielo: An Exploration of Latina/o Theatre for Young Audiences.* Dramatic Publishing Company, 2018.

García-Romero, Anne. *The Fornes Frame: Contemporary Latina Playwrights and the Legacy of Maria Irene Fornes.* University of Arizona Press, 2016.

Herrera, Brian Eugenio. *Latin Numbers: Playing Latino in Twentieth-Century U.S. Popular Performance.* University of Michigan Press, 2015.

Herrera, Patricia. *Nuyorican Feminist Performance: From the Café to Hip Hop Theater.* University of Michigan Press, 2020.

Huerta, Jorge. *Chicano Drama.* Cambridge University Press, 2000.

Rossini, Jon D. *Contemporary Latina/o Theater: Wrighting Ethnicity.* Southern Illinois University Press, 2008.

Santana, Analola, and Jimmy Noriega. *Theatre and Cartographies of Power: Repositioning the Latina/o Americas.* Southern Illinois University Press, 2018.

Schroeder-Arce, Roxanne. "Representations of Latinos/as in Musical Theater and Theater for Young Audiences," in *Latinos and American Popular Culture,* edited by P. M. Montilla, 189–210. Praeger, 2019.

Ybarra, Patricia. *Latinx Theater in the Times of Neoliberalism.* Northwestern University Press, 2017.

# SHAKING UP THE WORLD

## Latinx Teen Activists

Valentine's Day, in Parkland, Florida will likely never hold the same meaning as it does for many of us who mark February 14 as a day to celebrate the bonds of romantic love. That's because, on February 14, 2018, seventeen-year-old Nikolas Cruz, armed with a semiautomatic rifle, entered the grounds of his former high school, Marjory Stoneman Douglas, and killed almost 20 students and faculty members (Chuck). That this brutally violent act occurred on Valentine's Day is perhaps not the biggest tragedy; instead, for many adolescents living across this land, school shootings are no longer a rarity but an all-too-real possibility that has made active shooter drills another part of high school like fire drills used to be for us, Cristina and Trevor. Today's generation of teenagers has come of age in a century that has witnessed more active school shootings than at any time in our nation's history. In fact, after automobile accidents, the leading cause of death for young people is firearms ("16 Facts").

Outraged by the U.S. government's failure to enact gun legislation and by the Trump administration's courting of the NRA, the survivors of the Marjory Stoneman Douglas mass shooting spearheaded a nationwide march and rally, "March for Our Lives," a mere month after this tragedy. On March 24, 2018, teen activists took to the streets, making inspiring, highly emotional speeches that demanded action and critically called out our adult leaders for kowtowing to a gun lobby that has played a part in killing their friends and classmates. Since the march, the organizers have created an organization of the same name, whose mission is "to harness the power of young people across the country to fight for sensible gun violence prevention policies that save lives," according to their website. Defying the problematic myth that adults are solely responsible for invoking change, these teenagers have taken matters into their own hands.

One standout activist and Parkland survivor is Emma González, a self-identified Cuban, bisexual teenager who wrote an op-ed less than two weeks after the shooting and declared, "We are tired of practicing school shooter drills and feeling scared of something we should never have to think about. We are tired of being ignored. So we are speaking up for those who don't have anyone listening to them, for those who can't talk about it just yet, and for those who will never speak again" (González). The activists we chronicle in this chapter challenge the social, cultural, and political authority bestowed on adults, which all but erases youth as enactors of change. As scholar Jessica K. Taft explains: "Young people also continue to be seen by policy makers and other adults primarily as objects of public or civil policy, not as subjects to be engaged in its formation" (49). These young activists thus defy the expectations that we should simply allow the adults to "take charge." We'll discuss González's inspiring words that are intimately connected to her reality as a queer Latina adolescent later in this conclusion to document the ways that Latinx teenagers have shaken up our world for the better. We're inspired by her, and we have much to learn from young people like her who turn their trauma into action against a social system that is killing adolescents when they are doing the most "normal" thing—attending high school.

This terrible reality hit close to home for Trevor on January 14, 2020, when the high school he teaches at, Bellaire, in Houston, became the location of another senseless act of gun violence. Earlier that day, Trevor and his students had filmed a segment for *Localish* about their collaborative work using dance and social media to build relationships and stronger classroom communities. Yet the joy and laughter that filled Trevor's classroom soon turned sour when a student accidentally shot and killed his friend and classmate, Cesar Cortes, a nineteen-year-old ROTC student who had already enlisted in the Army. His life was over before it began, before he would get to live the dream of serving his country that he had had since he was a young boy. During perhaps the lowest point in his teaching career, Trevor saw firsthand the power of young activists. Like many Title 1 schools, the Bellaire High School ROTC program is composed primarily of Black and Brown students. And, in this moment of grief and anger, Trevor witnessed the resilience of his Latinx students, who advocated on behalf of their friend who would still be here if not for a senseless act of gun violence.

The role of these young Latinx activists has not occurred in a vacuum. Throughout this book we have explored the significant role that Latinx teenagers play in contemporary U.S. popular culture. The examples that fill these pages, from *Real Women Have Curves* and *On My Block* to *The Poet X* and *Swimming While Drowning*, speak to the ways that mainstream media conjures, forges, and illustrates teenage Latinidades. Although our focus has admittedly been on the lived realities of fictional Latinx teens, we conclude this book by shifting the focus to those inspiring Latinx teenagers who haven't just talked the talk but who have walked the walk. Just as we opened this conclusion with the work of Emma González and her Marjory Stoneman Douglas classmates, we recognize the labor of teenage activists Ramon Contreras, Sage Grace Dolan-Sandrino, and Latinx TikTokers. Similar to the ways that fictional teens such as Miles Morales and Victor Salazar institutionalize Latinidad, these real-life teens demonstrate how teenage Latinx identities already *are* the mainstream. There is no waiting around; the time is now. Latinx youth contribute to U.S. popular culture while their identities provide a roadmap to better understand representation, visibility, and the nuances of Latinidad. These teens are rewriting the narrative and declaring to the world, "This is what a Latinx teenager looks like."

## Emma González

It's safe to say that, if you're compared to the Cuban revolutionary leader José Martí, that makes you a pretty big deal. And while some would question how, exactly, a self-identified bisexual, Cubana teen with buzzed hair could be likened to the famed revolucionario, merely to call Emma González an activist is an understatement. Instead, González has become a household name for her inspiring, fierce activism that shuns politeness and silence. Indeed, when their high school classmates are murdered in their own school and their local, state, and federal legislators continue to receive funds from the gun lobby, how could we expect students like González to remain silent and deferential to their adult leaders? González's stature is even more significant when we consider how, according to Taft, there remains scant attention to teenage girls as activists and world changers (4). González's fearless, awe-inspiring words and actions should serve as a stark reminder to adult leaders that her brave activism should not have to exist in the first place. If American teens were not killed on a daily basis in their country, we would not need the courageous leadership of young people like Emma González.

In an article about González, New York University professor Ana Maria Dopico describes the teen activist as an icon of Cuban American history, indeed high praise: "As someone who has written about José Martí, who was a teenager when he became a political prisoner and went on to be a poet and political star, watching Emma González is absolutely fascinating. . . . Her open-hearted self-exposure, the mourning over martyred friends, the claim for youth as leaders of history, the call to the future, the remaking of citizenship, all these are part of Cuban and U.S. political history" (Morales). In addition, Taft's study of teen girl activists is crucial for reminding us that "girlhood is not an irrelevant social category, but one that is important to global capital and global citizenship, and, therefore, to our understandings of political resistance and social movements in the Americas" (6). In the days and months after the famous speech she gave at the March for Our Lives, she would amass more Twitter followers than the NRA (Morales), and her shaved head would become a symbol of youth activist resistance. Of course, prior to the February 2018 mass shooting at her high school, González was not an international teen icon. But even before she reached international fame, González *was* a key figure in her high school, an active participant in their Pride festivities and an organizer of a Valentine Day's fundraiser at her school just hours before the six minutes and twenty seconds of a mass shooting spree would change the course of her life forever.

For us, it is González's brilliant speech that marks her as an iconic figure of Latinx adolescent history and a standout moment in anti-gun violence activism more generally. Perhaps what is most powerful about her speech is what she does not say. For over six minutes, González bravely stands in silence in front of thousands of people in Washington, D.C., symbolizing the amount of time it took Cruz to murder her friends and teachers. With a tearstained, defiant face and donning a green bomber jacket with stickers declaring "WE CALL BS" and "I will vote," González declares, "for those who still can't comprehend because they refuse to, I'll tell you where it went, right into the ground, six feet deep. Six minutes and 20 seconds with an AR 15 and my friend Carmen would never complain to me about piano practice" (Rev.com). By invoking silence to mark the passage of time, González channels her trauma and rage to make a stunning display of visual political commentary.

In interviews and op-eds, González has honestly and tragically explained how the mass shooting traumatized her period of adolescence that was cut brutally short. Writing for *Harper's Bazaar* less than two weeks after the mass shooting, she begins her essay with, "My Name is Emma González. I'm 18 years old, Cuban and bisexual. I'm so indecisive that I can't pick a favorite color, and I'm allergic to 12 things. I draw, paint, crochet, sew, embroider—anything productive I can do with my hands while watching Netflix. But none of this matters anymore" (Gonzalez). While making visible her intersectional identity, what stands out equally is her suggestion that adolescence, a time of drawing, painting, and discovering the world, is a thing of the past. Importantly, González's words convey the reality that impacts many teens across this country—gun violence, an act that should not be normalized but is tragically too common. But we insist on highlighting her activism and her revolutionary status as part and parcel of Latinx adolescence. Teenagers like Emma González deserve a better world than the one adults have carved for them. Perhaps it's time for chiseling away at social problems to be left to the leaders, the teens of this world.

Ramon Contreras

June 2, 2018 began like any other humid summer day in New York City. But this day was different. Thousands of teenage gun-control activists donning the signature orange apparel of the gun reform movement defiantly marched throughout the city's five boroughs, even crossing the famed Brooklyn Bridge, in a protest against gun violence. The organizer? Then eighteen-year-old Afro-Latino Ramon Contreras, who led the procession as a pallbearer carrying a white coffin that symbolized those whom we have lost from preventable acts of gun violence. The march, Youth Over Guns, used grassroots organizing in addition to some added star power from March for Our Lives NYC and celebrities such as Julianne Moore and Susan Sarandon. Youth Over Guns has since morphed into a youth-led group led entirely by students of color who, similar to Emma González and the students of Marjory Stoneman Douglas, are tired of waiting for adults, specifically those in power, to make change. As Contreras knows firsthand, he doesn't need to wait around for anyone; he already has the power to enact change.

For Contreras, the issue of gun violence is close to home. Growing up in Harlem, gun violence was ever present, eventually leading to one of his friends being shot and killed. After the tragic death, Contreras dedicated his life to advocating for gun reform in communities of color. As he knows, gun violence is systemic and closely tied to socioeconomic realities far beyond the average person's control. Contreras admits, "Some of the roots, it goes to a lack of funding, and lack of effort towards our public school educational system and lack of funding towards local gun violence prevention groups who work on this issue for years now and work on the ground with students, and they are getting the funding and attention that they need" (Barner). Contreras's words reveal that, despite being young, he is most definitely not waiting on the sidelines for adults to take over.

Contreras's efforts, much like those of Emma González, convey the need for more young Latinx voices to be centered in the movement to address gun violence. In an interview with C-Span, Contreras paid homage to the Black and Brown civil rights leaders of the 1960s and 70s who fought for equality. Contreras has studied these prior movements, learning valuable strategies to get—and hold—people's attention on issues that are typically left out of the mainstream media. While the fight for equality and inclusion is sadly still very much a fight that is unfolding, young gun reform activists now recognize that gun violence is central to this challenge. Until gun violence is addressed, the movement toward equality will not be a viable reality.

It must be noted that, with the exception of Emma González, much of the media attention post-Parkland, Florida largely centered around the activism of white students. Contreras recognizes this, and his astute understanding of how gun violence disproportionately impacts communities of color simultaneously demonstrates the reality that these same communities are seldom credited with invoking real change around issues like gun legislation. As both a teenager and Latinx community member, Contreras argues, "when I traveled the country and connected white privileged Parkland kids with students from underserved communities affected by gun violence, I saw an immediate possibility for affected communities to work with served communities and unite for this one goal" (Zilber). Beyond his passion for gun violence activism, Contreras understands that real, political change requires that we "connect voting to real issues that underserved communities experience" (Zilber). This straightforward yet thoughtful understanding of how politics works makes Contreras not simply a potential leader; he already is a leader, yet he is a figure that few people may know. Because of his lack of both racial and economic privilege, the significant role he has played in advocating for voting enfranchisement and sensible gun legislation has been overlooked and erased. The reality is that the history of activism in this country was by and large led by communities of color, including teens like Ramon Contreras. As part of this rich history, we know Contreras will continue to be a history-maker in the future.

## Sage Grace Dolan-Sandrino

Since we began teaching decades ago, one thing has been abundantly clear—teenage activists are the future. They are some of the most passionate (not to mention powerful) activists in our communities. Take Sage Grace Dolan-Sandrino (2000–), for example. Dolan-Sandrino is a trans Afro-Latinx artist and community organizer who has always considered activism to be a core part of her life. "For me, an Afro-Latina trans girl and artist, activism is inherent in my existence. It's no longer a singular identifier. It's everyday life, it's art, it's community. It gives me hope," she explains (Dolan-Sandrino). At just thirteen years old, she began to transition but was met with resistance from her school's administration and was eventually outed at school. She was bullied and was even the victim of violence due to being trans. Yet, demonstrating her resilience (and general fierceness), Dolan-Sandrino took this experience and decided to change the system to reimagine schools as places where it's okay to be trans and out. She dedicated her life to becoming the activist that she needed when she was just starting to come of age. She knew that what she experienced didn't have to be what other trans teens experienced. She could change the narrative, and change the narrative she did.

In the process, she quickly became an activist with a significant public profile. While still in high school, she was an ambassador to the White House's initiative for Educational Excellence for African Americans, a member of the Kennedy Center Youth Council, and a member of the Gender Spectrum National Youth Council. Dolan-Sandrino's work has been featured in BET and *Vogue,* among other media outlets. She is widely considered to be one of the leading voices in Gen Z. She isn't just the future; she is the present.

Like so many case studies from *Latinx Teens,* November 8, 2016 proved to be a turning point in Dolan-Sandrino's life. After Donald Trump was elected president, she further situated herself as a leading voice in the LGBTQ+ community by speaking out against the Trump administration's systematic efforts to reduce the rights of the trans community. Her fight included organizing a walkout at her high school, which saw thousands of her classmates march in protest alongside her. She even became a regular contributor to *Teen Vogue,* where she advocated for gender equality and trans rights under the Trump administration.

In 2020, Dolan-Sandrino founded TEAM Mag, a creative studio and digital zine. Mirroring Dolan-Sandrino's identity markers and values, TEAM mag is Afro-Caribbean run, femme run, and queer run. Simply put, she is creating a type of safe space to engage in creative activism for young people just like herself. She is being the change she wishes to see in the world. Dolan-Sandrino adds, "Authentic representation is one of the most important things to focus on when telling a story. We are going to change the world as we know it" (Qtd. in Pellot).

Like so many activists in Gen Z, Instagram has been essential to her activist work. Instagram is the primary home of TEAM Mag. Instagram has enabled her to find other likeminded young people, to organize, and to build momentum. When the Black Lives Matter movement experienced a new wave of energy following the murders of Ahmaud Arbery, Breonna Taylor, and George Floyd set against the backdrop of the COVID-19 pandemic, traditional community organizing methods were thrown into disarray. And although this was potentially a challenge for activists who cut their teeth before social media, for teen activists like Dolan-Sandrino, having social media in her toolkit enabled her work to transcend the moment. As Dolan-Sandrino recognizes in an op-ed in *Vogue*, "Now we're mobilizing in a way that has never been possible." Other queer teens of color now have a space just for them to build their work while expanding their creative communities. As Dolan-Sandrino's work shows, the possibilities are endless with teens running the show.

## Latinx Teen TikTokers

On October 11, 2020, Olympic gold medalist and gymnast Laurie Hernandez did what so many members of Generation Z do on a daily basis—she made a TikTok. But this wasn't just any TikTok. Hernandez helped usher in a definitively Latina trend on the social media platform to celebrate Alexandria Ocasio-Cortez's thirty-first birthday. The TikTok challenge in question featured Hernandez putting on makeup to the sounds of AOC's now-famous speech on the floor of the House of Representatives in July 2020 in which she called out Florida Republican congressman Ted Yoho's misogynistic actions toward her. The soundscape of Hernandez's video features parts of AOC's speech remixed with Kendrick Lamar's 2017 song "Humble." As AOC's voice explains how Yoho called her "crazy," "disgusting," and "a fucking bitch," Laurie Hernandez lip-synchs, becoming one with AOC, while applying makeup, complete with AOC's signature bright red lipstick. The short video ends with Hernandez's AOC transformation as the congresswoman declares, "I am here because I have to show my parents that I am their daughter and that they did not raise me to accept abuse from men." This forceful speech was the mic drop all young women of color needed to hear, but especially those young people who daily face sexist catcalls, unwanted sexual attention, and harassment.

Although Hernandez had just turned twenty years old a few months before and was no longer a teenager, she gave credibility to the emerging AOC TikTok challenge, encouraging thousands of her teenage Latina fans to follow in her footsteps, not to mention in AOC's footsteps, as well. Hernandez's caption notes, "I had to do it. I wonder how AOC feels knowing most of gen z thinks she's iconic?" Just as the fictional Elena on *Diary of a Future President* looks up to the Latina Florida state senator, Hernandez and millions of teenage girls, many of them Latinas, look up to AOC. And why wouldn't they admire a fierce, whip-smart congressional leader who represents them and who proudly talks about her past life as a bartender who was struggling to pay rent and student loans? So iconic has AOC become that her lipstick, Stila's "Beso" shade, has become popularized and representative of all things badass, powerful, and feminist.

The AOC Birthday Challenge is just one example of how Latinx teens today have used TikTok in ways that go far beyond simple entertainment and joy scrolling. Since entering the U.S. market in 2018, TikTok has quickly become *the* social media app of choice for Gen Z. TikTok is a site for creativity and self-expression. TikTok is as synonymous with Gen Z as malls, arcades, and roller rinks were with Gen X teens and AOL Instant Messenger and MySpace were with Millennials. These are places we flock to in order to be around other like-minded people, to have fun, and to feel a sense of belonging. And, as Boffone proposes in *Renegades: Digital Dance Cultures from Dubsmash to TikTok*, "Digital spaces such as Dubsmash and TikTok allow Zoomers—and especially teens of color—to produce cultural content that, in turn, facilitates young people's participation in an increasingly inclusive and democratized media culture" (12). As such, TikTok serves as an integral place for Gen Z to shape inclusive, generational cultures. Hernandez's TikTok, for example, has accumulated over 2.7 million views, not to mention any potential views on other social media platforms such as Instagram, Twitter, and Facebook. Hernandez's AOC tribute was shared over 4,600 times, leading to over 11,000 videos in which teenage girls perform AOC's definitively Latina feminist vision for the future of the United States, a future in which young women aren't just seen as someone's wife or daughter, as Representative Yoho claimed in his apology speech, but rather a future in which women have agency and autonomy. In AOC's United States, Latina teens don't have to be defined by their relationships to the men in their lives.

As Latinx teens (re)claim space, digital platforms such as TikTok remain critical. Although many adults will continue to overlook and dismiss TikTok, teenagers recognize the power it holds not just to entertain but to express identity and build community.

## Onward and Upward

Just like the representative films, television shows, novels, and plays that fill the pages of this book, the real-life Latinx teens in this brief conclusion are only the tip of the iceberg. These teen phenoms are quite literally updating the narrative on Latinidad in the twenty-first century, offering us blueprints to better understand the myriad ways that Latinx teens have moved far beyond one-dimensional representations of teenage Latinidad. These teens, whether fictional or not, conjure issues that directly concern adolescents living in the United States today. On the page, stage, screen, and in real life, Latinx adolescents teach us the importance of fighting for one's dreams and claiming one's space in communities and spaces that exclude them. Daring to exist in a world that refuses to take teenagers seriously, these Latinx youth trailblazers are a force, proving that adolescents will change up and shake up our world for the better.

# WORKS CITED

"16 Facts About Gun Violence and School Shootings." *Sandy Hook Promise*, https:// www.sandyhookpromise.org/gun-violence/16-facts-about-gun-violence-and-school -shootings/. Accessed 20 Nov. 2020.

Abad, Erika. "Revisiting Naya Rivera's Santana Lopez: The Afro-Latina Who Deserved More Time." *Latinx Spaces*. 15 July 2020 https://www.latinxspaces.com/latinx-film/revisiting -naya-riveras-santana-lopez-the-afro-latina-who-deserved-more-time. Accessed 20 Nov. 2020.

Acevedo, Elizabeth. *The Poet X.* HarperTeen, 2018.

Acosta, Grisel Y. "Returning to the Bronx: Gender, the Outsider Perspective, and Utopia in *Juliet Takes a Breath.*" *Latina Outsiders Remaking Latina Identity*, edited by Grisel Y. Acosta. Routledge, 2019, pp. 88–94

Aguirre Darancou, Iván Eusebio. "There is no 'I' in *Trollhunters*: Gendered and Collective Heroism in Guillermo Del Toro's Multimedial Saga." *Latinx Ciné in the Twenty- First Century*, edited by Frederick Luis Aldama, University of Arizona Press, 2019, pp. 405–23.

Alamillo, Laura, Larissa Mercado-López, and Cristina Herrera, editors. *Voices of Resistance: Interdisciplinary Approaches to Chican@ Children's Literature.* Rowman and Littlefield, 2017.

Albertalli, Becky, creator. *Leah on the Offbeat.* New York, Balzer + Bray, 2018.

Albertalli, Becky, creator. *Love, Creekwood.* New York, Balzer + Bray, 2020.

Albertalli, Becky, creator. *Simon vs. the Homo Sapiens Agenda.* New York, Balzer + Bray, 2015.

Albertalli, Becky, creator. *The Upside of Unrequited.* New York, Balzer + Bray, 2017.

Albertalli, Becky, and Adam Silvera. *What If It's Us.* HarperTeen, 2018.

Aldama, Arturo. "Decolonizing Predatory Masculinities in *Breaking Bad* and *Mosquita y Mari.*" *Decolonizing Latinx Masculinities*, edited by Arturo Aldama and Frederick Luis Aldama, The University of Arizona Press, 2020, pp 117–30.

Aldama, Frederick Luis. *Latinx Superheroes in Mainstream Comics.* The University of Arizona Press, 2017.

Aldama, Frederick Luis. "Love, Victor: Brown Queer TVLandia Watershed; Or Hollywood Brown Flavored Bubblegum." *LatinxSpaces*, 29 July 2020, https://www.latinxspaces .com/latinx-film/love-victor-brown-queer-teen-tvlandia-watershed-or-hollywood -brown-flavored-bubblegum. Accessed 10 Nov 2020.

Aldama, Frederick Luis. *The Routledge Companion to Latina/o Popular Culture*. Routledge, 2016.

Aldama, Frederick Luis, and Christopher González. *Reel Latinxs: Representation in U.S. Film and TV*. The University of Arizona Press, 2019.

Aldama, Frederick Luis, and William Anthony Nericcio. *Talking #browntv: Latinas and Latinos on the Screen*. Ohio State University Press, 2019.

@BenjaminASaenz. "Ari & Dante came from a silent space that lives inside of me, an aging man. I wrote & I was a boy in love again. Two boys climbed out of my wounded heart—and now they belong more to my readers than they belong to me. It makes me sad and makes me happy too," *Twitter*, 24 July 2020, https://twitter.com/borderpoet/status/1286612141596868610.

Alonso, Carolina. "'The Coming-of-Age Experience in Chicanx Queer Novels *What Night Brings* and *Aristotle and Dante Discover the Secrets of the Universe*." *Nerds, Goths, Geeks, and Freaks: Outsiders in Chicanx and Latinx Young Adult Literature*, edited by Trevor Boffone and Cristina Herrera, University Press of Mississippi, 2020, pp. 175–89.

Anders, Allison, director. *Mi Vida Loca*. Channel Four Films, 1993.

Angeles, Cruz, director. *Don't Let Me Drown*. Parts and Labor, 2009.

Aptaker, Isaac, and Elizabeth Berger, creators. *Love, Victor*. 20th Television and The Walk-Up Company, 2020.

Asian American Performers Action Coalition (AAPAC). *Ethnic Representation on New York City Stages 2014-2015*, 2016. www.aapanyc.org/uploads/1/1/9/4/11949532/aapac_2014 -2015_report.pdf.

Azar, Assi, creator. *The Beauty and the Baker*. Endemol Israel for Keshet Broadcasting, 2020.

Baez, Jillian M. *In Search of Belonging: Latinas, Media, and Citizenship*. University of Illinois Press, 2018.

Baker, Andy, and Charlie Covell, creators. *End of the F***ing World*. Netflix, 2017–19.

Barner, Katherine. "Youth Gun Control Activists Journeyed Across the Brooklyn Bridge for 'Youth Over Guns' March." *Complex*. 2 June 2018, https://www.complex.com/life/2018/06/youth-gun-control-activists-brooklyn-bridge-youth-over-guns-march. Accessed 23 Nov. 2020.

Beltrán, Mary C. *Latina/o Stars in U.S. Eyes: The Making and Meanings of Film and TV Stardom*. University of Illinois Press, 2009.

Bobrick, Sam, creator. *Saved by the Bell*. NBC Productions and Peter Engel Productions, 1989–92.

Bochco, Steven, and David E. Kelley, creators. *Doogie Howser, M.D.* 20th Century Fox Television, 1989–93.

Boffone, Trevor. "Alexis Scheer." *50 Playwrights Project*. 14 May 2018, https://50playwrights .org/2018/05/14/alexis-scheer/.

Boffone, Trevor. "FAQs: *Swimming While Drowning* by Emilio Rodriguez." *50 Playwrights Project*, 4 Apr. 2017, https://50playwrights.org/2017/04/04/faqs-swimming-while -drowning-by-emilio-rodriguez//.

Boffone, Trevor. "Immigration Remains Pressing Issue in *Real Women Have Curves* at Dallas Theater Center." *Arts+Culture Texas*, 12 April 2019, http://artsandculturetx.com/immigration-remains-pressing-issue-in-real-women-have-curves-at-dallas-theater -center/.

Boffone, Trevor. *Renegades: Digital Dance Cultures from Dubsmash to TikTok*. Oxford University Press, 2021.

Boffone, Trevor. "Young, Gay, and Latino: 'Feeling Brown' in Emilio Rodriguez's *Swimming While Drowning*." *Nerds, Goths, Geeks, and Freaks: Outsiders in Chicanx and Latinx*

*Young Adult Literature*, edited by Trevor Boffone and Cristina Herrera, University Press of Mississippi, 2020, pp. 145–58.

Boffone, Trevor, and Cristina Herrera, editors. *Nerds, Goths, Geeks & Freaks: Outsiders in Chicanx and Latinx Young Adult Literature.* University Press of Mississippi, 2020.

Borowitz, Andy, and Susan Borowitz, creators. *The Fresh Prince of Bel-Air.* NBC Productions, 1990–6.

Bowman, Emma, and Lulu Garcia-Navarro. "Peter Ramsey Put The 1st Afro-Latino Spider-Man On Screen. It May Win Him An Oscar." *NPR.* 24 Feb. 2019, https://www.npr.org/2019/02/24/697117295/peter-ramsey-put-the-1st-afro-latino-spider-man-on-screen-it-may-win-him-an-oscar.

Broadway League. "The Broadway League Reveals 'The Demographics of the Broadway Audience' For 2017-2018 Season." *Broadway League.* 18 Oct. 2018, https://www.broadwayleague.com/press/press-releases/the-broadway-league-reveals-the-demographics-of-the-broadway-audienc-for-20172018-season/.

Byrge, Duane. "*Mosquita y Mari*: Sundance Film Review." *The Hollywood Reporter*, 26 Jan. 2012, https://www.hollywoodreporter.com/review/mosquita-y-mari-sundance-film-review-285176. Accessed 27 July 2020.

Cardoso, Patricia, director. *Real Women Have Curves.* HBO Films, 2002.

@carmencitalova. "I know this: Naya Rivera fought like hell for Santana Lopez's coming out story. And seeing an Afro-Latina come out to her Abuela gave me the courage to do the same. And coming out literally changed everything in my life. How can I ever say thank you? Saying goodbye? Impossible ♥." *Twitter*, 13 July 2020, https://twitter.com/carmencitaloves/status/1282790925622804482?s=20.

Carolei, Joseph, creator. *The All New Mickey Mouse Club.* Blue Wave Industries, Les Chousc Company, Steve Clements Productions, and Walt Disney Television, 1989–95.

Castillo, Monica. "TV has a new kind of heroine: The Latina genius. Here's why it matters." *Los Angeles Times*, 26 Feb. 2020, https://www.latimes.com/entertainment-arts/tv/story/2020-02-26/netflix-expanding-universe-ashley-garcia-disney-diary-future-president. Accessed 15 Sept. 2021.

Chávez, Linda Yvette, and Marvin Lemus, creators. *Gentefied*, 2020.

Chuck, Elizabeth, Alex Johnson, and Corky Siemaszko. "17 killed in mass shooting at high school in Parkland, Florida." NBC, 14 Feb 2018, https://www.nbcnews.com/news/us-news/police-respond-shooting-parkland-florida-high-school-n848101. Accessed 20 Nov. 2020.

Cisneros, Sandra. *The House on Mango Street.* Vintage, 1984, 2009.

Cohen, Rob, director. *The Fast and the Furious.* Universal Pictures, 2001.

Contreras, Ramon. "March for Our Lives Bus Tour." *C-SPAN.* 2 Aug. 2018, https://www.c-span.org/video/?449683-1/student-gun-violence-activists-participate-march-lives-bus-tour. Accessed 23 Nov. 2020.

Daniels, Greg, and Michael Schur, creators. *Parks and Recreation.* Deedle-Dee Productions and Universal Media Studios, 2015.

De Oliveira, Eddie. *Lucky.* Scholastic, 2004.

Delara, Youssef, and Michael D. Olmos, directors. *Filly Brown.* Cima Productions, Olmos Productions, and Silent Giant Entertainment, 2012.

Denby, David. "Big Loser, Small Winner." *The New Yorker.* 31 March 2003, https://www.newyorker.com/magazine/2003/03/31/big-loser-small-winner. Accessed 24 July 2020.

Denworth, Lydia. "The Outsize Influence of Your Middle-School Friends." *The Atlantic.* 28 Jan. 2020, https://www.theatlantic.com/family/archive/2020/01/friendship-crucial-adolescent-brain/605638/. Accessed 24 July 2020.

Dolan-Sandrino, Sage Grace. "Sage Grace Dolan-Sandrino on Hope." *Vogue*. 26 Aug. 2020, https://www.vogue.com/article/sage-grace-dolan-sandrino-the-state-of-hope. Accessed 19 Nov. 2020.

Durso, Laura E., and Gary J. Gates. "Serving Our Youth: Findings from a National Survey of Service Providers Working with Lesbian, Gay, Bisexual, and Transgender Youth Who Are Homeless or At Risk of Becoming Homeless." *The Williams Institute*, UCLA School of Law, July 2012, https://www.ojp.gov/ncjrs/virtual-library/abstracts/serving-our-youth-findings-national-survey-service-providers.

Ellis, Amanda. "Chicana Teens, Zines, and Poetry Scenes: *Gabi, A Girl in Pieces* by Isabel Quintero." *Nerds, Goths, Geeks, and Freaks: Outsiders in Chicanx/Latinx Young Adult Literature*, edited by Trevor Boffone and Cristina Herrera. University Press of Mississippi, 2020, pp. 15–30.

"Emma Gonzalez's powerful March for Our Lives speech in full." *YouTube*, uploaded by Guardian News, 24 March 2020, https://www.youtube.com/watch?v=u46HzTGVQhg.

"Emma Gonzalez March for Our Lives Speech Transcript." 24 March 2018. https://www.rev.com/blog/transcripts/emma-gonzalez-march-for-our-lives-speech-transcript. Accessed 23 Nov. 2020.

Esquibel, Catriona Rueda. *With Her Machete in Her Hand: Reading Chicana Lesbians*. University of Texas Press, 2006.

Esquivel, Ramon. "Latinx Theatre for Young Audiences: Where We Are and Where We Must Go." *HowlRound*, 8 Jan. 2019, https://howlround.com/latinx-theatre-young-audiences.

Famuyiwa, Rick, director. *Dope*. Significant Productions, i am OTHER, and Revolt Films, 2015.

@finelinelesbian. "THIS was the scene that changed my life. Naya made it feel so real & genuine. I used to watch this on repeat as a young closeted lesbian so that I would feel less alone. I knew that if I came out, I would be disowned/kicked out." *Twitter*. 13 July 2020, https://twitter.com/finelinelesbian/status/1282761561480798210?s=20.

Fisher, Lang, and Mindy Kaling, creators. *Never Have I Ever*. Netflix, 2021.

Fregoso, Rosa Linda. *The Bronze Screen: Chicana and Chicano Film Culture*. University of Minnesota Press, 1993.

Fregoso, Rosa Linda. "Twenty-First-Century Latinx Ciné: A Coda." *Latinx Ciné in the Twenty-First Century*, edited by Frederick Luis Aldama, The University of Arizona Press, 2019, pp. 483–85.

García, Enrique. "The Latina Superheroine: Protecting the Reader from the Comic Book Industry's Racial, Gender, Ethnic, and Nationalist Biases." *Comics Studies Here and Now*, edited by Frederick Luis Aldama, Routledge, 2018, pp. 163–78.

García, Marilisa Jimenez. "Side-by-Side: At the Intersections of Latinx Studies and ChYA-Lit." *The Lion and the Unicorn*, vol. 41, no. 1, 2017, pp. 113–22.

García-Crespo, Naida. "Caribbean Transnational Films and National Culture, or How Puerto Rican or Dominican Can You Be in 'Nueba Yol'"? *Centro Journal*, vol. 28, no. 1, 2016, pp. 146–75.

Garza, Adolfo. *Dragonlinked*. CreateSpace Independent Publishing Platform, 2013.

Garza, Adolfo. *The Bond: Dragonlinked Chronicles Volume 2*. CreateSpace Independent Publishing Platform, 2014.

Gates, Gary J. "How Many People Are Lesbian, Gay, Bisexual and Transgender?"

Gay, Roxane. "Review of *Juliet Takes a Breath* by Gabby Rivera." *Goodreads*, 1 Feb. 2016, https://www.goodreads.com/en/book/show/28648863-juliet-takes-a-breath.

Gerber, Craig, creator. *Elena of Avalor*. Disney Channel/Disney Junior, 2016–18.

Glatzer, Richard, and Wash Westmoreland, directors. *Quinceañera*. Cinetic Media, 2006.

Goldberg, Lesley. "Party of Five' Reboot Canceled at Freeform." *The Hollywood Reporter*, 17 April 2020, https://www.hollywoodreporter.com/live-feed/party-five-reboot-canceled-at-freeform-1290647. Accessed 28 July 2020.

Gómez, Isaac. *I Am Not Your Perfect Mexican Daughter*. N.d.

González, Emma. "Parkland Student Opens Up About Her Fight for Gun Control." *Harper's Bazaar*, 26 Feb. 2018, https://www.harpersbazaar.com/culture/politics/a18715714/protesting-nra-gun-control-true-story/. Accessed 20 Nov. 2020.

González, Tanya, and Eliza Rodríguez y Gibson. *Humor and Latina/o Camp in* Ugly Betty: *Funny Looking*. Lexington Books, 2015.

Gramlich, John. "How border apprehensions, ICE arrests and deportations have changed under Trump." *Pew Research Center*, 2 March 2020, https://www.pewresearch.org/fact-tank/2020/03/02/how-border-apprehensions-ice-arrests-and-deportations-have-changed-under-trump/. Accessed 20 July 2020.

Greenwald, Todd J., creator. *Wizards of Waverly Place*. The Disney Channel, 2007–12.

Guerrero, Aurora, director. *Mosquita y Mari*. Indion Entertainment Group, 2012.

Hardwicke, Catherine, director. *Twilight*. Summit Entertainment, 2008.

Harnick, Chris (June 30, 2020). "Turns Out Love, Victor Felt Quite a Bit of Viewer Love on Hulu". E! Online. Archived from the original on July 1, 2020. https://www.eonline.com/news/1166338/turns-out-love-victor-felt-quite-a-bit-of-viewer-love-on-huluAccessed 1 July , 2020.

Helford, Bruce, George Lopez, and Robert Borden, creators. *George Lopez*. Warner Bros. Television, 2002–7.

Hench, Kevin, creator. *Mr. Iglesias*. Netflix, 2019.

@heredia_alej. "Naya Rivera's Santana was the first time I saw a queer Black Latinx person represented on any medium of art. She didn't have to be respectable, kind, loving, anything but who she was. For a queer Dominican kid growing up in The Bronx, that was liberating," *Twitter*, 14 July 2020, 9:14 a.m., https://twitter.com/Heredia_Alej/status/1283042116386643972?s=20.

@lauriehernandez_. "I had to do it. I wonder how AOC feels knowing most of gen z thinks she's iconic? (disclaimer to the parents: foul language.)" *TikTok*. 11 Oct. 2020, https://www.tiktok.com/@lauriehernandez_/video/6882581814410480902?referer_url=https%3A%2F%2Fwww.teenvogue.com%2F&referer_video_id=6882581814410480902. Accessed 18 Nov. 2020.

Herrera, Cristina. *ChicaNerds in Chicana Young Adult Literature: Brown and Nerdy*. Routledge, 2020.

Herrera, Cristina. "Seeking Refuge *Under the Mesquite*: Nature Imagery in Guadalupe Garcia McCall's Verse Novel." *Children's Literature Association Quarterly*, vol. 44, no 2, 2019, pp. 194–209.

Hess, Jared, director. *Napoleon Dynamite*. Fox Searchlight Pictures, Paramount Pictures, and MTV Films, 2004.

Holzman, Winnie, creator. *My So-Called Life*. The Bedford Falls Company and ABC Productions, 1994–95.

Horta, Silvio, and Fernando Gaitán, creators. *Ugly Betty*. Silent H Productions, 2006.

Hudes, Quiara Alegria, and Erin McKeown, writers. *Miss You Like Hell*. The Public Theatre, 2016.

Hughes Brothers, directors. *Menace II Society*. New Line Cinema, 1993.

Hughes, John, director. *Ferris Bueller's Day Off*. Paramount Pictures, 1986.

Hughes, John, director. *Sixteen Candles*. Universal Pictures, 1984.

Hughes, John, director. *The Breakfast Club*. Universal Pictures, 1985.

Human Rights Campaign, Ché Juan Gonzalez Ruddell-Tabisola, and Lake Research Partners. 2009. "At the Intersection: Race, Sexuality and Gender." *Human Rights Campaign*, http://www.hrc.org/resources/at-the-intersection-race-sexuality-and-gender/.

Huerta, Jorge. Foreword. *Palabras del Cielo: An Exploration of Latina/o Theatre for Young Audiences*. Compiled by Jose Casas and edited with Christina Marin, Dramatic Publishing Company, 2018, pp. 7–9.

Iungerich, Lauren, Eddie Gonzalez, and Jeremy Haft, creators. *On My Block*. Crazy Cat Lady Productions, 2018.

Jiménez-García, Marilisa. *Side by Side: US Empire, Puerto Rico, and the Roots of American Youth Literature and Culture*. University Press of Mississippi, 2021.

@JohnLeguizamo. "Why can't we Latinx have a piece of the pie? We are the largest ethnic group in America and missing as if we didn't exist!" *Twitter*, 28 July 2020, https://twitter.com/johnleguizamo/status/1288307040146907136?lang=en.

Johnson, Susan. *To All the Boys I Loved Before*. Overbrook Entertainment and Awesomeness Films, 2018.

Jordan, Kathleen, creator. *Teenager Bounty Hunters*. Netflix, 2020.

Kaplan, Gabe, Alan Sacks, and Peter Meyerson, creators. *Welcome Back, Kotter*. The Komack Company, Inc. and Wolper Productions, 1975–79.

Kellett, Gloria Calderon, and Mike Royce, creators. *One Day at a Time*. Act III Productions, GloNation Studios, Snowpants Productions, and Sony Pictures Television, 2017–20.

Kneen, Bonnie. "Neither Very Bi Nor Particularly Sexual: The Essence of the Bisexual in Young Adult Literature." *Children's Literature in Education*, 46, 2015, pp. 359–77.

Kurland, Seth, and Mario Lopez, creators. *The Expanding Universe of Ashley Garcia*. Netflix, 2020.

Kusama, Karen, director. *Girlfight*. Green/Renzi, 2000.

Kwapis, Ken, director. *The Sisterhood of the Traveling Pants*. Alcon Entertainment, 2005.

Landis, John, director. *Animal House*. Universal Pictures, 1978.

Levitan, Steven, and Christopher Lloyd, creators. *Modern Family*. ABC, 2009–20.

Lippman, Amy, and Christopher Keyser, creators. *Party of Five*. Sony Pictures Television, 2020.

Lopez, Josefina. "Untitled," interview by Jorge Huerta. 3 Oct. 1992. Box 110, Folder 13–14. Jorge Huerta Papers, MSS 142. Mandeville Special Collections Library, University of California, San Diego.

López, Tiffany Ana. "Introduction." *Growing up Chicana/o*. Avon Books, 1993.

López, Tiffany Ana. "Suturing Las Ramblas to East LA: Transnational Performances of Josefina López's *Real Women Have Curves*." *Performing the U.S. Latina and Latino Borderlands*, edited by Arturo Aldama, Chela Sandoval, and Peter J. Garcia, Indiana University Press, 2012, pp. 296–308.

Lorre, Chuck, and Steven Molaro. *Young Sheldon*. CBS, 2017–21.

Lotz, Amanda. "Textual (Im)Possibilities in the U.S. Post-Network Era: Negotiating Production and Promotion Processes on Lifetime's Any Day Now." *Critical Studies in Media Communication* vol. 21, no. 1, 2004, pp. 22–43.

NPR. "Lupe Ontiveros Proudly Portrayed Dozens of Maids." *NPR*. 27 July 2012.

March for Our Lives. Marchforourlives.com. Accessed 20 Nov. 2020.

Marin, Christina. "Reclamando Nuestros Derechos: Examining the Intersection between Latina/o Theatre for Young Audiences and Human Rights Education." *Palabras del Cielo: An Exploration of Latina/o Theatre for Young Audiences*, compiled by Jose Casas and edited with Christina Marin, Dramatic Publishing Company, 2018, pp. 66–81.

Marghitu, Stefania. *Teen TV*. Routledge, 2021.

Marrero, Maria Teresa. "*Real Women Have Curves*: The Articulation of Fat as a Cultural/Feminist Issue." *Ollantay Theater Magazine*, vol. 1, no. 1, 1993, pp. 61–70.

Matos, Angel Daniel. "A Narrative of a Future Past: Historical Authenticity, Ethics, and Queer Latinx Futurity in *Aristotle and Dante Discover the Secrets of the Universe*." *Children's Literature*, vol. 47, 2019, pp. 30–56.

Matos, Angel Daniel. "The Conversion of 'Paul': Cultural, Religious, and Sexual Negotiations in Alex Sanchez's *The God Box*." *Atenea: A Bilingual Journal of the Humanities and Social Sciences*, vol. 31, 2011, pp. 91–109.

McCall, Guadalupe García. *All the Stars Denied*. Lee and Low, 2018.

Mercello, Vince, director. *The Kissing Booth*. Komixx Entertainment, 2018.

Miranda, Lin-Manuel, writer. *Hamilton*. Richard Rodgers Theatre, 2015.

Miranda, Lin-Manuel, and Quiara Alegría Hudes. *In the Heights*. Applause Theatre & Cinema Books, 2013.

Molina-Guzmán, Isabel. *Latinas & Latinos on TV: Colorblind Comedy in the Post-racial Network Era*. The University of Arizona Press, 2018.

Monaghan, Whitney. "Not Just a Phase: Queer Girlhood and Coming of Age on Screen." *Girlhood Studies*, vol. 12, no. 1, 2019, pp. 98–113.

Morales, Ed. "Emma González is young, Cuban and bisexual. She's bringing all her identities to the gunfight." *The Lily*, 6 Mar. 2018, https://www.thelily.com/emma-gonzalez -is-young-cuban-and-bisexual-shes-bringing-all-of-her-identities-to-the-gunfight/. Accessed 18 Nov. 2020.

Moore, Yan, and Linda Schuyler, creators. *Degrassi*. Epitome Pictures and Bell Media, 2001–16.

Murphy, Ryan, Brad Falchuk, and Ian Brennan, creators. *Glee*. 20th Century Fox Television, 2009–15.

Narea, Nicole. "The Supreme Court just allowed Trump's expansion of deportations to go unchecked." *Vox*, 25 June 2020. https://www.vox.com/policy-and-politics/2020/6/25/ 21302168/supreme-court-immigration-trump-deportation-thuraissigiam. Accessed 23 July 2020.

Palos, Ari, director. *Precious Knowledge*. Dos Vatos Productions, 2011.

Peikert, Mark. "*Our Dear Dead Drug Lord* Goes to the Grave." *Playbill*. 7 Dec. 2019. https:// www.playbill.com/article/our-dear-dead-drug-lord-goes-to-the-grave.

Pellot, Emerald. "This 19-year-old Queer Activist Started a Creative Agency to Give a Platform to Other Young LGBTQIA+ Artists." *In the Know*. n.d, https://www.intheknow .com/2020/09/11/this-19-year-old-queer-activist-started-a-creative-agency-to-give-a -platform-to-other-young-lgbtqia-artists/.

Peña, Ilana, creator. *Diary of a Future President*. CBS Television Studios and I Can & I Will Productions, 2020.

Perez-Brown, Maria, creator, *Taina*. Nickelodeon Productions, 2001–2.

Popelnik, Rodolfo. "Changing Imaginaries Or The Importance of the Independent Indie for the Reconstruction of Caribbean Portrayals: The Case of *Raising Victor Vargas*." *Sargasso*, vol. 2, 2003–4, pp. 63–80.

Portugal, Carlos, and Kathleen Bedoya, creators. *East Los High*. Wise Entertainment, Population Media Center, Into Action Films, 2013–17.

Prado, Emily. "*I Am Not Your Perfect Mexican Daughter* is the Coming-of-Age Novel Chicana Teens Deserve." *Remezcla*, Oct. 2017, http://remezcla/features/culture/erika -sanchez-debut-novel/.

Ramírez Berg, Charles. *Latino Images in Film: Stereotypes, Subversion, and Resistance*. University of Texas Press, 2002.

Ramsey, Peter, director. *Spider-Man: Into the Spider-Verse*. Sony Pictures, 2018.

Remezcla Estaff. "What Latino Critics Are Saying About 'Spider-Man: Into the Spider-Verse.'" *Remezcla*. 12 Dec. 2018. https://remezcla.com/lists/film/latino-critics-review -spider-man-into-spider-verse/.

Rice-González, Charles. *Chulito*. Magnus Books, 2011.

Rich, Adrienne. "Compulsory Heterosexuality and Lesbian Existence." *The Lesbian and Gay Studies Reader*, edited by Henry Abelove, Michèle Aina Barale, and David M. Halperin, Routledge, 1993, pp. 227–54.

Rivadeneyra, Rocío. "Do You See What I See? Latino Adolescents' Perceptions of the Images on Television." *Journal of Adolescent Research*, vol. 21, no. 4, 2006, pp. 393–414.

Rivera, Gabby. *Juliet Takes a Breath*. Riverdale Avenue Books, 2016.

Rodriguez, Emilio. *Swimming While Drowning*. N.d.

Rodríguez, René. "First Love: That Magic Feeling." *Hispanic* vol. 16, no. 5, 2003, pp. 70.

Rodríguez, Richard T. "Impossible Mission: The Queer Geographies of Peter Bratt's *La Mission*." *Latinx Ciné in the Twenty-First Century*, edited by Frederick Luis Aldama, The University of Arizona Press, 2019, pp. 450–60.

Ross, Gary, director. *The Hunger Games*. Lionsgate, 2012.

Sáenz, Benjamin Alire. *Aristotle and Dante Discover the Secrets of the Universe*. Simon & Schuster, 2012.

Sáenz, Benjamin Alire. *Carry Me Like Water*. Rayo, 2005.

Sáenz, Benjamin Alire. *Everything Begins and Ends at the Kentucky Club*. Cinco Puntos Press, 2012.

Sanchez, Jenny Torres. *We Are Not From Here*. Penguin, 2020.

Sanchez, Alex. *Boyfriends with Girlfriends*. Simon and Schuster BFYR, 2011.

Sanchez Saltveit, Olga. "Ignited: *El Payaso* in Flint." *HowlRound*, 2 Feb. 2017. https://howlround.com/ignited.

Santos, Adrianna M. "Broken Open: Writing, Healing, and Affirmation in Isabel Quintero's *Gabi, a Girl in Pieces* and Erika L. Sanchez's *I Am Not Your Perfect Mexican Daughter*." *Nerds, Goths, Geeks, and Freaks: Outsiders in Chicanx and Latinx Young Adult Literature*, edited by Trevor Boffone and Cristina Herrera, University Press of Mississippi, 2020, pp. 45–59.

Saracho, Tanya, creator. *Vida*. Big Beach TV, 2018–20.

Scheer, Alexis. *Our Dear Dead Drug Lord*. n.d.

Schienberg, Jonathan, director. *Colossus*. Campanario Entertainment, 2018.

Schroeder-Arce, Roxanne. "Representations of Latinos/as in Musical Theater and Theater for Young Audiences." *Latinos and American Popular Culture*, edited by P.M. Montilla, Praeger, 2013, 189–210.

Schroeder-Arce, Roxanne. "Sin Fronteras: Latinx and Latin American Theatre for Young Audiences." *HowlRound*, 6 Jan. 2019, https://howlround.com/sin-fronteras.

Shafer, Jessie, and Rocío Rivadeneyra. "The Impact of Televised Stereotypes on the State Self-Esteem of Latino/a Emerging Adults: The Moderating Role of Ethnic-Racial Identity." *Emerging Adulthood*, 2020, pp. 1–7. DOI 21676968209213O. Web.

Shukert, Rachel, creator. *The Baby-Sitters Club*. Netflix, 2020–21.

Silvera, Adam. *History is All You Left Me*. Soho Teen, 2017.

Silvera, Adam. *Infinity Reaper*. Quill Tree Books, 2021.

Silvera, Adam. *Infinity Son*. HarperTeen, 2020.

Silvera, Adam. *More Happy Than Not*. Soho Teen, 2015.

Silvera, Adam. *They Both Die At the End*. HarperTeen, 2017.

Singleton, John, director. *Boyz n the Hood*. Columbia Pictures, 1991.

Smith, Stacy L., Marc Choueiti, and Dr. Katherine Pieper. "Inequality in 800 Popular Films: Examining Portrayals of Gender, Race/Ethnicity, LGBT, and Disability from 2007–2015," Media, Diversity, and Social Change Initiative, USC Annenberg and Annenberg Foundation, 2016.

Snyder Urman, Jennie, creator. *Jane the Virgin*. Warner Bros. Television, 2014–19.

Sollett, Peter, director. *Raising Victor Vargas*. Canal, 2003.

Spitzer, Justin, creator. *Superstore*. Spitzer Holding Company, The District, and Universal Television, 2015.

Taft, Jessica K. *Rebel Girls: Youth Activism and Social Change Across the Americas*. New York University Press, 2010.

Trujillo, Carla. *What Night Brings*. Curbstone, 2003.

Viramontes, Helena María. *Under the Feet of Jesus*. Plume, 1996.

Weitz, Paul, director. *American Pie*. Universal Pictures, 1999.

The Williams Institute, April 2011, https://williamsinstitute.law.ucla.edu/publications/how -many-people-lgbt/.

Yandoli, Krystie Lee. "Netflix's 'On My Block' Brings Young People Of Color Into The Limelight — Finally, Cast Says." *Buzzfeed News*, 19 March 2018, https://www.buzzfeednews .com/article/krystieyandoli/on-my-block-representation-young-people-of-color.

Ye Hee Lee, Michelle. "Donald Trump's false comments connecting Mexican immigrants and crime." *Washington Post*, 8 July 2015, https://www.washingtonpost.com/news/ fact-checker/wp/2015/07/08/donald-trumps-false-comments-connecting-mexican -immigrants-and-crime/. Accessed 15 Sept. 2021.

York Jones, Ben, and Michael Mohan, creators. *Everything Sucks!* Netflix, 2018.

Yorkey, Brian, creator. *13 Reasons Why*. Netflix, 2017–20.

Zilber, Amelie. "Youth Activist Ramon Contreras Champions Minorities to Participate in Politics." *The Sunday Paper*, 11 Nov. 2018, https://mariashriver.com/youth-activist -ramon-contreras-champions-minorities-participate-politics/. Accessed 20 Nov. 2020.

# INDEX

**Trevor Boffone** is a Lecturer in the Women's, Gender & Sexuality Studies Program at the University of Houston and a high school Spanish teacher at Bellaire High School. His work using Dubsmash and TikTok with his students has been featured on Good Morning America, ABC News, Inside Edition, and Access Hollywood, among numerous national and local media platforms. He is the author of *Renegades: Digital Dance Cultures from Dubsmash to TikTok* (Oxford University Press, 2021). He is the co-editor of *Encuentro: Latinx Performance for the New American Theater* (Northwestern University Press, 2019); *Nerds, Goths, Geeks, and Freaks: Outsiders in Chicanx and Latinx Young Adult Literature* (University Press of Mississippi, 2020); *Shakespeare & Latinidad* (Edinburgh University Press, 2021); and *Seeking Common Ground: Latinx and Latin American Theatre and Performance* (Methuen Drama, 2021).

**Cristina Herrera** is Professor and Director of Chicano/Latino Studies at Portland State University. She earned her PhD in English from Claremont Graduate University in 2008. Herrera has authored and co-edited six books on Chicanx/Latinx literature. A trained literature scholar, she is author of *Contemporary Chicana Literature: (Re) Writing the Maternal Script* (Cambria Press, 2014) and *ChicaNerds in Chicana Young Adult Literature: Brown and Nerdy* (Routledge,

2020). Herrera is co-editor of *Voices of Resistance: Interdisciplinary Approaches to Chican@ Children's Literature* (Rowman & Littlefield, 2017) and *Nerds, Goths, Geeks, and Freaks: Outsiders in Chicanx and Latinx Young Adult Literature,* was published in 2020 by University Press of Mississippi. Herrera has also published articles in *Chicana/ Latina Studies, Critique: Studies in Contemporary Fiction, Children's Literature, The Lion and the Unicorn, Children's Literature Association Quarterly,* and other journals.